No 06

FLUTT
KIM by Kim Hargreaves

TWELVE
DESIGNS +ONE

designs & styling Kim Hargreaves
editor Kathleen Hargreaves
photographer Nicole Jopek
hair & make-up Laura Lawrence
model Holly Ardron
graphic design Lyndsay Kaye
pattern writer Sue Whiting
pattern checker Tricia McKenzie

ISBN 978-1-906487-36-2

© **Copyright Kim Hargreaves 2019. All Rights Reserved.**
First published in 2019 by Kim Hargreaves
printed by Lion FPG
No part of this book may be reproduced, distributed or transmitted in any form or by any means, including photcopying or other electronic or mechanical method, without prior written permission of the copy right owner, except in the case of breif quotations embodied in critical reviws and certain other non commercial uses permmitted by copyright law. The designs and illustrations in this publication are copyrighted and must not be knitted for re-sale. Yarn quantities are approximate as they are based on average requirements. Images are as close as printing will allow.

THANK YOU
We would like to say a huge thank you to our wonderful team; firstly Nicole for the most fabulous photographs, Laura for the stunning hair & make-up, Holly our very beautiful model, Lyndsay for great artwork, Sue and Tricia for their pattern writing and checking skills, Glenis, Heather, Karan, Sandra, Shona and Susan for their wonderful knitting & finishing, Neya, David, Sharon and the Rowan team for their continuing support, and finally Richard & all at Lion for printing the book & so much more.

KIM HARGREAVES
22 Broad Lane, Upperthong, Holmfirth, HD9 3JS, ENGLAND
www.kimhargreaves.co.uk / kim@kimhargreaves.co.uk

CONTENTS

the designs	06
the patterns	38
information page	62
index	64

FREE SPIRITED

A collection with an air of femininity and bohemian ease. The designs pretty, the shades ethereal, combined they create a harmonious mix to recharge and calm.

FLURRY knitted in kidsilk haze | the pattern on page 38

TIZZY knitted in summerlite dk | the pattern on page 40

WAVER knitted in creative linen   the pattern on page 56
FAIN knitted in creative linen   the pattern on page 53

WAVER knitted in creative linen | the pattern on page 56

GLIDE knitted in cotton cashmere | the pattern on page 42

LALA knitted in handknit cotton | the pattern on page 46

FLUTTER knitted in kidsilk haze : the pattern on page 44

QUIVER knitted in summerlite 4ply | the pattern on page 55

AYA knitted in handknit cotton | the pattern on page 50

NOVA knitted in summerlite dk | the pattern on page 57

ARIA knitted in creative linen . the pattern on page 60

EILA knitted in summerlite dk   the pattern on page 58

FAIN knitted in creative linen | the pattern on page 53

SWIRL knitted in handknit cotton & summerlite 4ply | the pattern on page 49

SWIRL knitted in handknit cotton & summerlite 4ply | the pattern on page 49

FLURRY ••
picture on page 08

THE PATTERN

	XS	S	M	L	XL	XXL	
To fit bust	**81**	**86**	**91**	**97**	**102**	**109**	**cm**
	32	34	36	38	40	43	in

ROWAN KIDSILK HAZE / Aura
8 9 9 10 10 11 x 25gm

NEEDLES
1 pair 4½mm (no 7) (US 7) needles
1 pair 6mm (no 4) (US 10) needles

TENSION
15 sts and 20 rows to 10 cm measured over stocking stitch using 6mm (US 10) needles and yarn DOUBLE.

BACK
Cast on 92 (96: 100: 106: 110: 116) sts using 4½mm (US 7) needles and yarn DOUBLE.
Row 1 (RS): P0 (1: 0: 0: 0: 0), K1 (2: 1: 0: 2: 1), *P2, K2, rep from * to last 3 (1: 3: 2: 0: 3) sts, P2 (1: 2: 2: 0: 2), K1 (0: 1: 0: 0: 1).
Row 2: K0 (1: 0: 0: 0: 0), P1 (2: 1: 0: 2: 1), *K2, P2, rep from * to last 3 (1: 3: 2: 0: 3) sts, K2 (1: 2: 2: 0: 2), P1 (0: 1: 0: 0: 1).
These 2 rows form rib.
Work in rib for a further 11 rows, ending with a **RS** row.
Row 14 (WS): Rib 1 (3: 5: 0: 2: 5), K2tog, *rib 6, K2tog, rep from * to last 1 (3: 5: 0: 2: 5) sts, rib 1 (3: 5: 0: 2: 5). 80 (84: 88: 92: 96: 102) sts.
Change to 6mm (US 10) needles.
Beg with a K row, now work in st st throughout as follows:
Cont straight until back measures 46 (46: 47: 47: 47: 47) cm, ending with a WS row.
Shape armholes
Place markers at both ends of last row (to denote base of armhole openings).
Work 6 rows.
Next row (RS): K3, M1, K to last 3 sts, M1, K3.
Working all armhole increases as set by last row, inc 1 st at each end of 8th and 3 (3: 3: 2: 1: 0) foll 8th rows, then on 0 (0: 0: 1: 2: 3) foll 10th rows. 90 (94: 98: 102: 106: 112) sts.
Work 7 (9: 9: 9: 9: 9) rows, ending with a WS row.
Shape shoulders and back neck
Cast off 5 (5: 6: 6: 6: 7) sts at beg of next 2 rows. 80 (84: 86: 90: 94: 98) sts.
Next row (RS): Cast off 5 (6: 6: 6: 7: 7) sts, K until there are 21 (21: 22: 23: 24: 26) sts on right needle and turn, leaving rem sts on a holder.
Work each side of neck separately.
Dec 1 st at neck edge of next 2 rows, then on foll alt row **and at same time** cast off 6 (6: 6: 6: 7: 7) sts at beg of 2nd row, then 6 (6: 6: 7: 7: 8) sts at beg of foll alt row.
Work 1 row.
Cast off rem 6 (6: 7: 7: 7: 8) sts.
With RS facing, rejoin yarn DOUBLE to rem sts, cast off centre 28 (30: 30: 32: 32: 32) sts, K to end.
Complete to match first side, reversing shapings.

LEFT FRONT
Cast on 51 (53: 55: 58: 60: 63) sts using 4½mm (US 7) needles and yarn DOUBLE.
Row 1 (RS): P0 (1: 0: 0: 0: 0), K1 (2: 1: 0: 2: 1), *P2, K2, rep from * to last 6 sts, K6.
Row 2: K6, P2, *K2, P2, rep from * to last 3 (1: 3: 2: 0: 3) sts, K2 (1: 2: 2: 0: 2), P1 (0: 1: 0: 0: 1).
These 2 rows set the sts – front opening edge 6 sts in g st with all other sts in rib.
Cont as set for a further 11 rows, ending with a **RS** row.
Row 14 (WS): K6, P2, K2tog, *rib 6, K2tog, rep from * to last 1 (3: 5: 0: 2: 5) sts, rib 1 (3: 5: 0: 2: 5). 45 (47: 49: 51: 53: 56) sts.
Change to 6mm (US 10) needles.
Next row (RS): Knit.
Next row: K6, P to end.
These 2 rows set the sts – front opening edge 6 sts still in g st with all other sts now in st st.
Cont as now set until 14 rows less have been worked than on back to armhole marker, ending with a WS row.
Shape front slope
Next row (RS): K to last 9 sts, K2tog tbl, K7.
Working all front slope decreases as set by last row, dec 1 st at front slope edge on 4th (4th: 4th: 2nd: 4th: 4th) and 2 foll 4th rows. 41 (43: 45: 47: 49: 52) sts.
Work 1 (1: 1: 3: 1: 1) rows, ending with a WS row.
Shape armhole
Place marker at end of last row (to denote base of armhole opening).
Working all armhole increases as set by back and keeping front slope decreases correct as set, dec 1 st at front slope edge of 3rd (3rd: 3rd: next: 3rd: 3rd) and 10 (11: 11: 12: 12: 12) foll 4th rows **and at same time** inc 1 st at armhole edge of 7th and 4 (4: 4: 3: 2: 1) foll 8th rows, then on 0 (0: 0: 1: 2: 3) foll 10th rows. 35 (36: 38: 39: 41: 44) sts.
Work 3 (1: 1: 1: 1: 3) rows, ending with a WS row.

FLURRY

Shape shoulder
Cast off 5 (5: 6: 6: 6: 7) sts at beg of next and foll 1 (0: 3: 2: 0: 2) alt rows, then 6 (6: 7: 7: 7: 8) sts at beg of foll 3 (4: 1: 2: 4: 2) alt rows **and at same time** dec 1 st at front slope edge of 3rd row. 6 sts.
Inc 1 st at end of next row. 7 sts.
Now working all sts in g st, cont on this set of 7 sts (for back neck border extension) until this strip measures 11 (11.5: 11.5: 12: 12: 12) cm, ending with a WS row.
Cast off.

RIGHT FRONT
Cast on 51 (53: 55: 58: 60: 63) sts using 4½mm (US 7) needles and yarn DOUBLE.
Row 1 (RS): K8, *P2, K2, rep from * to last 3 (1: 3: 2: 0: 3) sts, P2 (1: 2: 2: 0: 2), K1 (0: 1: 0: 0: 1).
Row 2: K0 (1: 0: 0: 0: 0), P1 (2: 1: 0: 2: 1), *K2, P2, rep from * to last 6 sts, K6.
These 2 rows set the sts – front opening edge 6 sts in g st with all other sts in rib.
Cont as set for a further 11 rows, ending with a **RS** row.
Row 14 (WS): Rib 1 (3: 5: 0: 2: 5), K2tog, *rib 6, K2tog, rep from * to last 8 sts, P2, K6. 45 (47: 49: 51: 53: 56) sts.
Change to 6mm (US 10) needles.
Next row (RS): Knit.
Next row: P to last 6 sts, K6.
These 2 rows set the sts – front opening edge 6 sts still in g st with all other sts now in st st.
Cont as now set until 14 rows less have been worked than on back to armhole marker, ending with a WS row.
Shape front slope
Next row (RS): K7, K2tog, K to end.
Working all front slope decreases as set by last row, complete to match left front, reversing shapings.

SLEEVES (both alike)
Cast on 48 (50: 52: 54: 54: 54) sts using 4½mm (US 7) needles and yarn DOUBLE.
Row 1 (RS): P1 (2: 3: 0: 0: 0), *K2, P2, rep from * to last 3 (0: 1: 2: 2: 2) sts, K2 (0: 0: 2: 2: 2), P1 (0: 1: 0: 0: 0).

Row 2: K1 (2: 3: 0: 0: 0), *P2, K2, rep from * to last 3 (0: 1: 2: 2: 2) sts, P2 (0: 0: 2: 2: 2), K1 (0: 1: 0: 0: 0).
These 2 rows form rib.
Work in rib for a further 11 rows, ending with a **RS** row.
Row 14 (WS): K1 (2: 3: 0: 0: 0), (P2, K2) 0 (0: 0: 1: 1: 0) times, *P1, yrn, P1, K2, rep from * to last 3 (0: 1: 2: 2: 2) sts, (P1, yrn) 1 (0: 0: 0: 0: 1) times, P1 (0: 0: 2: 2: 1), K1 (0: 1: 0: 0: 0).
60 (62: 64: 66: 66: 68) sts.
Change to 6mm (US 10) needles.
Beg with a K row, work in st st throughout as follows:
Work 2 rows, ending with a WS row.
Next row (RS): K3, M1, K to last 3 sts, M1, K3.
Working all increases as set by last row, inc 1 st at each end of 16th (16th: 24th: 18th: 14th: 12th) and every foll 16th (18th: 24th: 18th: 14th: 12th) row to 66 (72: 72: 74: 72: 76) sts, then on every foll 18th (-: -: 20th: 16th: 14th) row until there are 70 (-: -: 76: 78: 82) sts.
Cont straight until sleeve measures 47 (48: 49: 50: 51: 52) cm, ending with a WS row.
Cast off.

MAKING UP
Press all pieces with a warm iron over a damp cloth.
Join both shoulder seams using back stitch or mattress stitch if preferred. Join cast-off ends of back neck border extensions, then sew one edge to back neck. Sew cast-off edge of sleeves to back and fronts between markers denoting base of armhole openings. Join side and sleeve seams.

53.5 (56: 58.5: 61: 63.5: 67.5) cm
21 (22: 23: 24: 25: 26½) in

71 (72: 73: 74: 75: 76) cm
28 (28¼: 28¾: 29¼: 29½: 30) in

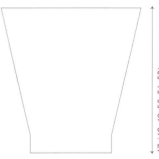

47 (48: 49: 50: 51: 52) cm
18½ (19: 19¼: 19¾: 20: 20½) in

TIZZY
picture on page 11

THE PATTERN

	XS	S	M	L	XL	XXL	
To fit bust	81	86	91	97	102	109	cm
	32	34	36	38	40	43	in

ROWAN SUMMERLITE DK / Silvery Blue

10 11 12 13 14 15 x 50gm

NEEDLES
1 pair 2¾mm (no 12) (US 2) needles
1 pair 3¼mm (no 10) (US 3) needles

TENSION
Based on an average tension of 25 sts and 34 rows to 10 cm using 3¼mm (US 3) needles.

SPECIAL ABBREVIATIONS
inc2 = make 3 sts from 1 st by working (K1, P1, K1) all into next st; **MB** = make bobble – see below for details; **Tw2L** = K into back of second st on left needle, then K first st and slip both sts off left needle together; **Tw2R** = K into front of second st on left needle, then K first st and slip both sts off left needle together.

Bobble note: Bobbles shown on photographed garment are worked as follows: (K1, yfwd, K1, yfwd, K1) all into next st, turn, P5, turn, K5, turn, P2tog, P1, P2tog, turn, sl 1, K2tog, psso.
When working next row, knit into the back of the bobble st.

Note: For a smaller bobble please see page 63.

BACK
Cast on 120 (126: 134: 140: 146: 158) sts using 2¾mm (US 2) needles.
Row 1 (RS): K1 (0: 0: 0: 0: 0), P2 (2: 2: 1: 0: 2), (K2, P2) 3 (4: 5: 6: 7: 8) times, *Tw2R, Tw2L, (P2, K2) 4 times, P2, Tw2R, Tw2L*, (P2, K2) 9 times, P2, rep from * to * once more, (P2, K2) 3 (4: 5: 6: 7: 8) times, P2 (2: 2: 1: 0: 2), K1 (0: 0: 0: 0: 0).
Row 2: P1 (0: 0: 0: 0: 0), K2 (2: 2: 1: 0: 2), (P2, K2) 3 (4: 5: 6: 7: 8) times, *P4, (K2, P2) 4 times, K2, P4*, (K2, P2) 9 times, K2, rep from * to * once more, (K2, P2) 3 (4: 5: 6: 7: 8) times, K2 (2: 2: 1: 0: 2), P1 (0: 0: 0: 0: 0).
Row 3: K1 (0: 0: 0: 0: 0), P2 (2: 2: 1: 0: 2), (K2, P2) 3 (4: 5: 6: 7: 8) times, *Tw2L, Tw2R, (P2, K2) 4 times, P2, Tw2L, Tw2R*, (P2, K2) 9 times, P2, rep from * to * once more, (P2, K2) 3 (4: 5: 6: 7: 8) times, P2 (2: 2: 1: 0: 2), K1 (0: 0: 0: 0: 0).
Row 4: As row 2.
Last 4 rows form fancy rib.
Work in fancy rib for a further 15 rows, ending with a **RS** row.
Row 20 (WS): P1 (0: 0: 0: 0: 0), (K2tog) 1 (0: 1: 0: 0: 0) times, P2 (0: 2: 0: 2: 0), K2 (2: 2: 1: 2: 2), (P2, K2tog, P2, K2) 1 (2: 2: 3: 3: 4) times, *P4, (K2, P2) twice, K2tog, (P2, K2) twice, P4*, (K2, P2) 4 times, K2, P1, M1, P1, K2, (P2, K2) 4 times, rep from * to * once more, (K2, P2, K2tog, P2) 1 (2: 2: 3: 3: 4) times, K2 (2: 2: 1: 2: 2), P2 (0: 2: 0: 2: 0), (K2tog) 1 (0: 1: 0: 0: 0) times, P1 (0: 0: 0: 0: 0). 115 (121: 127: 133: 139: 149) sts.
Change to 3¼mm (US 3) needles.
Now work in patt as follows:
Row 1 (RS): P1 (0: 1: 0: 1: 0), (P1, K1 tbl) 5 (7: 8: 10: 11: 14) times, *P2, Tw2R, Tw2L, work next 17 sts as row 1 of diamond panel, Tw2R, Tw2L, P2*, P35, rep from * to * once more, (K1 tbl, P1) 5 (7: 8: 10: 11: 14) times, P1 (0: 1: 0: 1: 0).
Row 2: K11 (14: 17: 20: 23: 28), *K2, P4, work next 17 sts as row 2 of diamond panel, P4, K2*, P3tog, (inc2, P3tog) 8 times, rep from * to * once more, K11 (14: 17: 20: 23: 28).
Row 3: P1 (0: 1: 0: 1: 0), (P1, K1 tbl) 5 (7: 8: 10: 11: 14) times, *P2, Tw2L, Tw2R, work next 17 sts as row 3 of diamond panel, Tw2L, Tw2R, P2*, P33, rep from * to * once more, (K1 tbl, P1) 5 (7: 8: 10: 11: 14) times, P1 (0: 1: 0: 1: 0).
Row 4: K11 (14: 17: 20: 23: 28), *K2, P4, work next 17 sts as row 4 of diamond panel, P4, K2*, inc2, (P3tog, inc2) 8 times, rep from * to * once more, K11 (14: 17: 20: 23: 28).
These 4 rows set the sts – 2 diamond panels with twist st braids each side, central blackberry st panel, and edge sts in textured patt. (**Note**: The number of sts varies whilst working central blackberry st panel. Count sts after patt rows 1 and 4 **only**. All st counts given presume there are 35 sts in central panel **at all times**.)
Keeping patts correct and repeating the 24 row diamond panel repeat throughout, cont as follows:
Cont in patt until work measures 30 (30: 31: 31: 31: 31) cm, ending with a WS row.
Shape armholes
Keeping patt correct, cast off 4 (4: 5: 5: 6: 6) sts at beg of next 2 rows.
107 (113: 117: 133: 127: 137) sts.
Dec 1 st at each end of next 3 (3: 5: 5: 7: 7) rows, then on foll 1 (3: 2: 3: 2: 5) alt rows, then on foll 4th row. 97 (99: 101: 105: 107: 111) sts.
Cont straight until armhole measures 19 (20: 20: 21: 22: 23) cm, ending with a WS row.
Shape shoulders and back neck
Keeping patt correct, cast off 7 (7: 7: 8: 8: 9) sts at beg of next 2 rows. 83 (85: 87: 89: 91: 93) sts.

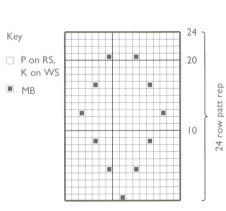

Key
□ P on RS, K on WS
■ MB

24 row patt rep

TIZZY

Next row (RS): Cast off 7 (7: 7: 8: 8: 9) sts, patt until there are 11 (11: 12: 11: 12: 12) sts on right needle and turn, leaving rem sts on a holder. Work each side of neck separately.
Cast off 4 sts at beg of next row.
Cast off rem 7 (7: 8: 7: 8: 8) sts.
With RS facing, rejoin yarn and cast off central sts until there are 17 (17: 18: 18: 19: 20) sts left on left needle (and one st on right needle), patt to end. 18 (18: 19: 19: 20: 21) sts.
Complete to match first side, rev shapings.

FRONT
Work as given for back until 24 (24: 24: 28: 28: 28) rows less have been worked than on back to start of shoulder shaping, ending with a WS row.
Shape front neck
Next row (RS): Patt 31 (32: 33: 35: 36: 38) sts, P4 (3: 3: 3: 3: 3) and turn, leaving rem sts on a holder. 35 (35: 36: 38: 39: 41) sts.
Work each side of neck separately.
Keeping patt correct, dec 1 st at neck edge of next 10 rows, then on foll 2 alt rows, then on 2 (2: 2: 3: 3: 3) foll 4th rows.
21 (21: 22: 23: 24: 26) sts.
Work 1 row, ending with a WS row.
Shape shoulder
Cast off 7 (7: 7: 8: 8: 9) sts at beg of next and foll alt row.
Work 1 row.
Cast off rem 7 (7: 8: 7: 8: 8) sts.
With RS facing, rejoin yarn and cast off central sts until there are 34 (34: 35: 37: 38: 40) sts left on left needle (and one st on right needle), patt to end. 35 (35: 36: 38: 39: 41) sts.
Complete to match first side, rev shapings.

SLEEVES (both alike)
Cast on 68 (70: 72: 76: 78: 80) sts using 2¾mm (US 2) needles.
Row 1 (RS): K0 (0: 1: 0: 0: 1), P1 (2: 2: 1: 2: 2), (K2, P2) 2 (2: 2: 3: 3: 3) times, Tw2R, Tw2L, (P2, K2) 10 times, P2, Tw2R, Tw2L, (P2, K2) 2 (2: 2: 3: 3: 3) times, P1 (2: 2: 1: 2: 2), K0 (0: 1: 0: 0: 1).
Row 2: P0 (0: 1: 0: 0: 1), K1 (2: 2: 1: 2: 2), (P2, K2) 2 (2: 2: 3: 3: 3) times, P4, (K2, P2) 10 times, K2, P4, (K2, P2) 2 (2: 2: 3: 3: 3) times, K1 (2: 2: 1: 2: 2), P0 (0: 1: 0: 0: 1).
Row 3: K0 (0: 1: 0: 0: 1), P1 (2: 2: 1: 2: 2), (K2, P2) 2 (2: 2: 3: 3: 3) times, Tw2L, Tw2R, (P2, K2) 10 times, P2, Tw2L, Tw2R, (P2, K2) 2 (2: 2: 3: 3: 3) times, P1 (2: 2: 1: 2: 2), K0 (0: 1: 0: 0: 1).
Row 4: As row 2.
Last 4 rows form fancy rib.
Work in fancy rib for a further 16 rows, inc 1 st at centre of last row and ending with a WS row. 69 (71: 73: 77: 79: 81) sts.
Change to 3¼mm (US 3) needles.
Now work in patt as follows:
Row 1 (RS): P1 (0: 1: 1: 0: 1), (P1, K1 tbl) 3 (4: 4: 5: 6: 6) times, P2, Tw2R, Tw2L, P43, Tw2R, Tw2L, P2, (K1 tbl, P1) 3 (4: 4: 5: 6: 6) times, P1 (0: 1: 1: 0: 1).
Row 2: K9 (10: 11: 13: 14: 15), P4, K2, P3tog, (inc2, P3tog) 9 times, K2, P4, K9 (10: 11: 13: 14: 15).
Row 3: P1 (0: 1: 1: 0: 1), (P1, K1 tbl) 3 (4: 4: 5: 6: 6) times, P2, Tw2L, Tw2R, P41, Tw2L, Tw2R, P2, (K1 tbl, P1) 3 (4: 4: 5: 6: 6) times, P1 (0: 1: 1: 0: 1).
Row 4: K9 (10: 11: 13: 14: 15), P4, K2, inc2, (P3tog, inc2) 9 times, K2, P4, K9 (10: 11: 13: 14: 15).
These 4 rows set the sts – central blackberry st panel with twist st braids each side, and edge sts in textured patt.
(**Note**: The number of sts varies whilst working central blackberry st panel. Count sts after patt rows 1 and 4 *only*. All st counts given presume there are 39 sts in central panel **at all times**.)
Keeping patts correct, cont as follows:
Inc 1 st at each end of next and every foll 4th (4th: 6th: 6th: 6th: 6th) row to 79 (77: 107: 101: 107: 105) sts, then on every foll 6th (6th: -: 8th: 8th: 8th) row until there are 103 (105: -: 109: 113: 115) sts, taking inc sts into textured patt.
Cont straight until sleeve measures 37 (38: 39: 40: 41: 42) cm, ending with a WS row.
Shape top
Keeping patt correct, cast off 4 (4: 5: 5: 6: 6) sts at beg of next 2 rows.
95 (97: 97: 99: 101: 103) sts.
Dec 1 st at each end of next 3 rows, then on every foll alt row until 77 sts rem, then on foll 7 rows, ending with a WS row. 63 sts.
Cast off 3 sts at beg of next 4 rows.
Cast off rem 51 sts.

MAKING UP
Press all pieces with a warm iron over a damp cloth.
Join right shoulder seam using back stitch or mattress stitch if preferred.
Neckband
With RS facing and using 2¾mm (US 2) needles, pick up and knit 26 (26: 26: 29: 29: 29) sts down left side of front neck, 26 (28: 28: 28: 28: 28) sts from front, 26 (26: 26: 29: 29: 29) sts up right side of front neck, and 52 (54: 54: 56: 56: 56) sts from back. 130 (134: 134: 142: 142: 142) sts.
Row 1 (WS): K2, *P2, K2, rep from * to end.
Row 2: P2, *K2, P2, rep from * to end.
These 2 rows form rib.
Work in rib for a further 6 rows, ending with a **RS** row.
Cast off in rib (on **WS**).
Join left shoulder and neckband seam. Join side seams. Join sleeve seams. Insert sleeves into armholes.

43 (45.5: 48: 50.5: 53: 57) cm
17 (18: 19: 20: 21: 22½) in

49 (50: 51: 52: 53: 54) cm
19¼ (19¾: 20: 20½: 21: 21¼) in

37 (38: 39: 40: 41: 42) cm
14½ (15: 15¼: 15¾: 16¼: 16½) in

GLIDE ..
picture on page 16

THE PATTERN

	XS	S	M	L	XL	XXL	
To fit bust	81	86	91	97	102	109	cm
	32	34	36	38	40	43	in

ROWAN COTTON CASHMERE / Silver Lining

6 7 7 8 8 9 x 50gm

NEEDLES
1 pair 3mm (no 11) (US 2/3) needles
1 pair 3¾mm (no 9) (US 5) needles

TENSION
22 sts and 28 rows to 10 cm measured over pattern using 3¾mm (US 5) needles.

BACK
Cast on 113 (123: 128: 138: 143: 153) sts using 3mm (US 2/3) needles.
Row 1 (RS): K8, *P2, K3, rep from * to last 5 sts, K5.
Row 2: K5, P3, *K2, P3, rep from * to last 5 sts, K5.
These 2 rows set the sts – 5 sts in g st at each end of row and all other sts in rib.
Cont as set for a further 15 rows, ending with a **RS** row.
Row 18 (WS): K5, rib 8 (3: 8: 3: 8: 8), K2tog, (P3, K2tog) 17 (21: 20: 24: 23: 25) times, rib 8 (3: 8: 3: 8: 8), K5. 95 (101: 107: 113: 119: 127) sts.
Work in g st for 6 rows, ending with a WS row.
Change to 3¾mm (US 5) needles.
Now work in patt as follows:
Row 1 (RS): Knit.
Row 2: Purl.
Rows 3 to 6: As rows 1 and 2 twice.
Row 7: Purl.
Row 8: Knit.
Rows 9 to 12: As rows 7 and 8 twice.
Row 13: K to end, winding yarn twice round needle for every st.
Row 14: P to end, dropping extra loops of previous row.
Rows 15 to 20: As rows 7 and 8, 3 times.
These 20 rows form patt.
Cont in patt until back measures 29 (29: 30: 30: 30: 30) cm, ending with a WS row.
Shape armholes
Keeping patt correct, cast off 4 (4: 5: 5: 6: 6) sts at beg of next 2 rows.
87 (93: 97: 103: 107: 115) sts.
Dec 1 st at each end of next 3 (3: 5: 5: 7: 7) rows, then on foll 2 (4: 3: 5: 4: 6) alt rows, then on foll 4th row. 75 (77: 79: 81: 83: 87) sts.
Cont straight until armhole measures 18 (19: 19: 20: 21: 22) cm, ending with a WS row.
Shape shoulders and back neck
Cast off 7 (7: 7: 7: 8: 8) sts at beg of next 2 rows. 61 (63: 65: 67: 67: 71) sts.
Next row (RS): Cast off 7 (7: 7: 7: 8: 8) sts, patt until there are 11 (11: 12: 12: 11: 13) sts on right needle and turn, leaving rem sts on a holder.
Cast off 4 sts at beg of next row.
Cast off rem 7 (7: 8: 8: 7: 9) sts.
With RS facing, rejoin yarn to rem sts, cast off centre 25 (27: 27: 29: 29: 29) sts, patt to end.
Complete to match first side, reversing shapings.

LEFT FRONT
Cast on 49 (54: 54: 59: 64: 69) sts using 3mm (US 2/3) needles.
Row 1 (RS): K8, *P2, K3, rep from * to last st, K1.
Row 2: P4, *K2, P3, rep from * to last 5 sts, K5.
These 2 rows set the sts – 5 sts in g st at side seam edge and all other sts in rib.
Cont as set for a further 15 rows, ending with a **RS** row.
Row 18 (WS): Rib 4 (4: 14: 14: 4: 4), K2tog, (P3, K2tog) 6 (8: 5: 7: 9: 10) times, rib 8 (3: 8: 3: 8: 8), K5. 42 (45: 48: 51: 54: 58) sts.
Work in g st for 6 rows, ending with a WS row.
Change to 3¾mm (US 5) needles.
Beg with row 1, now work in patt as given for back as follows:
Cont straight until left front matches back to start of armhole shaping, ending with a WS row.
Shape armhole
Keeping patt correct, cast off 4 (4: 5: 5: 6: 6) sts at beg of next row. 38 (41: 43: 46: 48: 52) sts.
Work 1 row.
Dec 1 st at armhole edge of next 3 (3: 5: 5: 7: 7) rows, then on foll 2 (4: 3: 5: 4: 6) alt rows, then on foll 4th row. 32 (33: 34: 35: 36: 38) sts.
Cont straight until 18 (18: 18: 20: 20: 20) rows less have been worked than on back to start of shoulder shaping, ending with a WS row.
Shape front neck
Next row (RS): Patt 29 (29: 30: 31: 32: 34) sts, cast off rem 3 (4: 4: 4: 4: 4) sts.
Rejoin yarn with **WS** facing and cont as follows:
Dec 1 st at neck edge of next 4 rows, then on foll 3 (3: 3: 4: 4: 4) alt rows, then on foll 4th row. 21 (21: 22: 22: 23: 25) sts.
Work 3 rows, ending with a WS row.

GLIDE

Shape shoulder
Cast off 7 (7: 7: 7: 8: 8) sts at beg of next and foll alt row.
Work 1 row. Cast off rem 7 (7: 8: 8: 7: 9) sts.

RIGHT FRONT
Cast on 49 (54: 54: 59: 64: 69) sts using 3mm (US 2/3) needles.
Row 1 (RS): K4, *P2, K3, rep from * to last 5 sts, K5.
Row 2: K5, P3, *K2, P3, rep from * to last st, P1.
These 2 rows set the sts – 5 sts in g st at side seam edge and all other sts in rib.
Cont as set for a further 15 rows, ending with a **RS** row.
Row 18 (WS): K5, rib 8 (3: 8: 3: 8: 8), K2tog, (P3, K2tog) 6 (8: 5: 7: 9: 10) times, rib 4 (4: 14: 14: 4: 4). 42 (45: 48: 51: 54: 58) sts.
Complete to match left front, reversing shapings and working first row of neck shaping as follows:
Shape front neck
Next row (RS): Cast off 3 (4: 4: 4: 4: 4) sts, patt to end. 29 (29: 30: 31: 32: 34) sts.

SLEEVES (both alike)
Cast on 68 (72: 74: 76: 78: 82) sts using 3mm (US 2/3) needles.
Row 1 (RS): K3 (0: 1: 2: 3: 0), *P2, K3, rep from * to last 5 (2: 3: 4: 5: 2) sts, P2, K3 (0: 1: 2: 3: 0).
Row 2: P3 (0: 1: 2: 3: 0), *K2, P3, rep from * to last 5 (2: 3: 4: 5: 2) sts, K2, P3 (0: 1: 2: 3: 0).
These 2 rows form rib.
Cont in rib for a further 15 rows, ending with a **RS** row.
Row 18 (WS): P3 (0: 1: 2: 3: 0), *K2tog, P3, rep from * to last 5 (2: 3: 4: 5: 2) sts, K2tog, P3 (0: 1: 2: 3: 0). 55 (57: 59: 61: 63: 65) sts.
Work in g st for 6 rows, ending with a WS row.
Change to 3¾mm (US 5) needles.
Beg with row 1, now work in patt as given for back as follows:
Inc 1 st at each end of 3rd and 4 (4: 4: 4: 2: 2) foll 10th (10th: 10th: 10th: 8th: 8th) rows, then on 2 (2: 2: 2: 5: 5) foll 12th (12th: 12th: 12th: 10th: 10th) rows, taking inc sts into patt. 69 (71: 73: 75: 79: 81) sts.

Cont straight until sleeve measures approx 36 (36: 37: 37: 37: 37) cm, ending after same patt row as on back to start of armhole shaping and with a WS row.
Shape top
Keeping patt correct, cast off 4 (4: 5: 5: 6: 6) sts at beg of next 2 rows. 61 (63: 63: 65: 67: 69) sts.
Dec 1 st at each end of next 3 rows, then on foll alt row, then on 3 foll 4th rows.
47 (49: 49: 51: 53: 55) sts.
Work 1 row.
Dec 1 st at each end of next and every foll alt row until 41 sts rem, then on foll 7 rows, ending with a WS row.
Cast off rem 27 sts.

MAKING UP
Press all pieces with a warm iron over a damp cloth.
Join both shoulder seams using back stitch or mattress stitch if preferred.
Left front band
With RS facing and using 3mm (US 2/3) needles, pick up and knit 90 (90: 94: 94: 98: 98) sts evenly down entire left front opening edge, from neck shaping to cast-on edge.
Work in g st for 4 rows, ending with a **RS** row.
Row 1 (WS): K3, P3, *inc knitwise in next st, P3, rep from * to end.
111 (111: 116: 116: 121: 121) sts.
Row 2: *K3, P2, rep from * to last 6 sts, K6.
Row 3: K3, P3, *K2, P3, rep from * to end.
Last 2 rows set the sts – hem edge 3 sts in g st with all other sts in rib.
Cont as now set for a further 7 rows, ending with a **RS** row.
Cast off in patt (on **WS**).
Right front band
With RS facing and using 3mm (US 2/3) needles, pick up and knit 90 (90: 94: 94: 98: 98) sts evenly up entire right front opening edge, from cast-on edge to neck shaping.
Work in g st for 4 rows, ending with a **RS** row.
Row 1 (WS): *P3, inc knitwise in next st, rep from * to last 6 sts, P3, K3.
111 (111: 116: 116: 121: 121) sts.

Row 2: K6, *P2, K3, rep from * to end.
Row 3: *P3, K2, rep from * to last 6 sts, P3, K3.
Last 2 rows set the sts – hem edge 3 sts in g st with all other sts in rib.
Cont as now set for a further 7 rows, ending with a **RS** row.
Cast off in patt (on **WS**).
Neckband
With RS facing and using 3mm (US 2/3) needles, beg and ending at cast-off edges of front bands, pick up and knit 10 sts across top of front band, 3 (4: 4: 4: 4: 4) sts from neck cast-off, 21 (21: 21: 23: 23: 23) sts up right side of front neck, 33 (35: 35: 37: 37: 37) sts from back, 21 (21: 21: 23: 23: 23) sts down left side of front neck, 3 (4: 4: 4: 4: 4) sts from neck cast-off, and 10 sts across top of front band. 101 (105: 105: 111: 111: 111) sts.
Work in g st for 6 rows, ending with a **RS** row.
Cast off knitwise (on **WS**).
Join side seams, leaving seams open for first 24 rows (for side seam openings). Join sleeve seams. Insert sleeves into armholes.

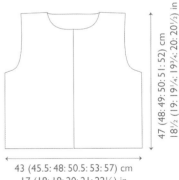

47 (48: 49: 50: 51: 52) cm
18½ (19: 19¼: 19¾: 20: 20½) in

43 (45.5: 48: 50.5: 53: 57) cm
17 (18: 19: 20: 21: 22½) in

35 (36: 37: 38: 39: 40) cm
13¾ (14¼: 14½: 15: 15¼: 15¾) in

FLUTTER
picture on page 21

THE PATTERN

	XS	S	M	L	XL	XXL
To fit bust	81	86	91	97	102	109 cm
	32	34	36	38	40	43 in

ROWAN KIDSILK HAZE / Ghost

4 5 5 5 6 6 x 25gm

NEEDLES
1 pair 2¾mm (no 12) (US 2) needles
1 pair 3¼mm (no 10) (US 3) needles

TENSION
25 sts and 34 rows to 10 cm measured over stocking stitch using 3¼mm (US 3) needles.

BACK
Cast on 102 (108: 114: 120: 126: 136) sts using 2¾mm (US 2) needles and yarn **DOUBLE**.
Break off one strand of yarn and complete back using one strand of yarn **only** throughout.
Work in g st for 16 rows, ending with a WS row.
Change to 3¼mm (US 3) needles.
Next row (RS): Knit.
Next row: K6, P to last 6 sts, K6.
These 2 rows set the sts – 6 sts still in g st at each end of rows and all other sts now in st st.
Keeping sts correct as now set, cont as follows:
Work 18 (18: 20: 20: 20: 20) rows, ending with a WS row.
Next row (RS): K12, K2tog, K to last 14 sts, K2tog tbl, K12.
Working all side seam decreases as set by last row, cont as follows:
Work 7 rows, dec 1 st at each end of 6th of these rows and ending with a WS row. 98 (104: 110: 116: 122: 132) sts.
Place markers at both ends of last row (to denote top of side seam openings).
Now working **all** sts in st st, cont as follows:
Dec 1 st at each end of 5th and 3 foll 6th rows. 90 (96: 102: 108: 114: 124) sts.
Work 15 (15: 17: 17: 17: 17) rows, ending with a WS row.**
Next row (RS): K3, M1, K to last 3 sts, M1, K3.
Working all side seam increases as set by last row, inc 1 st at each end of 8th and foll 8th row, then on 3 foll 10th rows.
102 (108: 114: 120: 126: 136) sts.
Work 11 rows, ending with a WS row.
Shape armholes
Cast off 5 (5: 6: 6: 7: 7) sts at beg of next 2 rows. 92 (98: 102: 108: 112: 122) sts.
Dec 1 st at each end of next 1 (3: 3: 5: 5: 7) rows, then on foll 2 (2: 3: 2: 3: 4) alt rows, then on 2 foll 4th rows.
82 (84: 86: 90: 92: 96) sts.
Cont straight until armhole measures 18 (19: 19: 20: 21: 22) cm, ending with a WS row.

Shape shoulders and back neck
Cast off 7 (7: 8: 8: 8: 9) sts at beg of next 2 rows. 68 (70: 70: 74: 76: 78) sts.
Next row (RS): Cast off 7 (7: 8: 8: 8: 9) sts, K until there are 12 (12: 11: 12: 13: 13) sts on right needle and turn, leaving rem sts on a holder.
Cast off 4 sts at beg of next row.
Cast off rem 8 (8: 7: 8: 9: 9) sts.
With RS facing, rejoin yarn to rem sts, cast off centre 30 (32: 32: 34: 34: 34) sts, K to end.
Complete to match first side, reversing shapings.

FRONT
Work as given for back to **.
Working side seam increases in same way as given for back, inc 1 st at each end of next and 2 foll 8th rows, then on foll 10th row. 98 (104: 110: 116: 122: 132) sts.
Work 7 rows, ending with a WS row.
Divide for front neck
Next row (RS): K46 (49: 52: 55: 58: 63), K2tog tbl, K1 and turn, leaving rem sts on a holder. 48 (51: 54: 57: 60: 65) sts.
Work each side of neck separately.
Work 3 rows, inc 1 st at side seam edge of 2nd of these rows and ending with a WS row. 49 (52: 55: 58: 61: 66) sts.
Next row (RS): K to last 3 sts, K2tog tbl, K1.
Working all neck decreases as set by last row, dec 1 st at neck edge of 4th and 3 foll 4th rows **and at same time** inc 1 st at side seam edge of 8th row.
45 (48: 51: 54: 57: 62) sts.
Work 3 rows, ending with a WS row.
Shape armhole
Cast off 5 (5: 6: 6: 7: 7) sts at beg and dec 1 st at end of next row.
39 (42: 44: 47: 49: 54) sts.
Work 1 row.
Dec 1 st at armhole edge of next 1 (3: 3: 5: 5: 7) rows, then on foll 2 (2: 3: 2: 3: 4) alt rows, then on 2 foll 4th rows **and at same time** dec 1 st at neck edge of 3rd and 2 (3: 3: 3: 4: 5) foll 4th rows.
31 (31: 32: 34: 34: 35) sts.

FLUTTER

Dec 1 st at neck edge **only** on 2nd (4th: 2nd: 2nd: 4th: 4th) and 5 (6: 6: 7: 4: 2) foll 4th rows, then on 3 (2: 2: 2: 4: 5) foll 6th rows.
22 (22: 23: 24: 25: 27) sts.
Cont straight until front matches back to start of shoulder shaping, ending with a WS row.
Shape shoulder
Cast off 7 (7: 8: 8: 8: 9) sts at beg of next and foll alt row.
Work 1 row.
Cast off rem 8 (8: 7: 8: 9: 9) sts.
With RS facing, rejoin yarn to rem sts, K1, K2tog, K to end. 48 (51: 54: 57: 60: 65) sts.
Complete to match first side, reversing shapings.

SLEEVES (both alike)
Cast on 53 (55: 57: 61: 63: 65) sts using 3¼mm (US 3) needles and yarn DOUBLE.
Break off one strand of yarn and complete sleeve using one strand of yarn **only** thoughout.
Beg with a K row, work in st st throughout as follows:
Work 12 rows, ending with a WS row.
Next row (RS): K3, M1, K to last 3 sts, M1, K3.
Working all increases as set by last row, inc 1 st at each end of 10th (10th: 10th: 12th: 12th: 12th) and every foll 10th (10th: 10th: 12th: 12th: 12th) row to 69 (67: 65: 75: 89: 87) sts, then on every foll 12th (12th: 12th: 14th: -: 14th) row until there are 79 (81: 83: 85: -: 91) sts.
Cont straight until sleeve measures 47 (48: 49: 50: 51: 52) cm, ending with a WS row.
Shape top
Cast off 5 (5: 6: 6: 7: 7) sts at beg of next 2 rows. 69 (71: 71: 73: 75: 77) sts.
Dec 1 st at each end of next 3 rows, then on foll 2 alt rows, then on 4 foll 4th rows.
51 (53: 53: 55: 57: 59) sts.
Work 1 row.
Dec 1 st at each end of next and every foll alt row until 45 sts rem, then on foll 7 rows, ending with a WS row. 31 sts.
Cast off 3 sts at beg of next 2 rows.
Cast off rem 25 sts.

MAKING UP
Press all pieces with a warm iron over a damp cloth.
Join right shoulder seam using back stitch or mattress stitch if preferred.
Neckband
With RS facing and using 2¾mm (US 2) needles, pick up and knit 76 (78: 78: 81: 84: 86) sts down left side of front neck, place marker on needle, pick up and knit 76 (78: 78: 81: 84: 86) sts up right side of front neck, and 38 (40: 40: 42: 42: 42) sts from back.
190 (196: 196: 204: 210: 214) sts.
Row 1 (WS): K to within 2 sts of marker, K2tog, slip marker onto right needle, K2tog tbl, K to end.
Row 2: K to within 2 sts of marker, K2tog tbl, slip marker onto right needle, K2tog, K to end.
Rep last 2 rows 3 times more, ending with a **RS** row. 174 (180: 180: 188: 194: 198) sts.
Join in second strand of yarn.
Using yarn DOUBLE, cast off knitwise (on **WS**), still decreasing either side of marker as before.
Join left shoulder and neckband seam.
Join side seams, leaving seams open below markers (for side seam openings). Join sleeve seams. Insert sleeves into armholes.

40.5 (43: 45.5: 48: 50.5: 54.5) cm
16 (17: 18: 19: 20: 21½) in

57 (58: 59: 60: 61: 62) cm
22½ (23: 23¼: 23¾: 24: 24½) in

47 (48: 49: 50: 51: 52) cm
18½ (19: 19¼: 19¾: 20: 20½) in

LALA •••
picture on page 19

THE PATTERN

	XS	S	M	L	XL	XXL	
To fit bust	81	86	91	97	102	109	cm
	32	34	36	38	40	43	in

ROWAN HANDKNIT COTTON / Feather
18 19 19 20 21 22 x 50gm

NEEDLES
1 pair 3mm (no 11) (US 2/3) needles
1 pair 3¾mm (no 9) (US 5) needles

BUTTONS – 6

TENSION
24 sts and 30 rows to 10 cm measured over blackberry stitch using 3¾mm (US 5) needles.

SPECIAL ABBREVIATIONS
inc2 = make 3 sts from 1 st by working (K1, P1, K1) all into next st; **MB** = make bobble – see below for details; **Tw2L** = K into back of second st on left needle, then K first st and slip both sts off left needle together; **Tw2R** = K into front of second st on left needle, then K first st and slip both sts off left needle together.

Bobble note: Bobbles shown on photographed garment are worked as follows: (K1, yfwd, K1, yfwd, K1) all into next st, turn, P5, turn, K5, turn, P2tog, P1, P2tog, turn, sl 1, K2tog, psso.
When working next row, knit into the back of the bobble st.

Note: For a smaller bobble please see page 63.

BACK
Cast on 118 (124: 130: 136: 142: 152) sts using 3mm (US 2/3) needles.
Row 1 (RS): K0 (1: 0: 0: 0: 0), P0 (2: 2: 1: 0: 1), (K2, P2) 5 (5: 6: 7: 8: 9) times, *Tw2R, Tw2L, P2, (K2, P2) 4 times, Tw2R, Tw2L*, P2, (K2, P2) 6 times, rep from * to * once more, (P2, K2) 5 (5: 6: 7: 8: 9) times, P0 (2: 2: 1: 0: 1), K0 (1: 0: 0: 0: 0).
Row 2: P0 (1: 0: 0: 0: 0), K0 (2: 2: 1: 0: 1), (P2, K2) 5 (5: 6: 7: 8: 9) times, *P4, K2, (P2, K2) 4 times, P4*, K2, (P2, K2) 6 times, rep from * to * once more, (K2, P2) 5 (5: 6: 7: 8: 9) times, K0 (2: 2: 1: 0: 1), P0 (1: 0: 0: 0: 0).
Row 3: K0 (1: 0: 0: 0: 0), P0 (2: 2: 1: 0: 1), (K2, P2) 5 (5: 6: 7: 8: 9) times, *Tw2L, Tw2R, P2, (K2, P2) 4 times, Tw2L, Tw2R*, P2, (K2, P2) 6 times, rep from * to * once more, (P2, K2) 5 (5: 6: 7: 8: 9) times, P0 (2: 2: 1: 0: 1), K0 (1: 0: 0: 0: 0).
Row 4: As row 2.
Last 4 rows form fancy rib.
Work in fancy rib for a further 15 rows, ending with a **RS** row.
Row 20 (WS): P0 (1: 0: 0: 0: 0), K0 (2: 2: 1: 0: 1), (P2, K2) 5 (5: 6: 7: 8: 9) times, *P4, (K2, P2) twice, K2tog, (P2, K2) twice, P4*, K2, (P2, K2tog) 5 times, P2, K2, rep from * to * once more, (K2, P2) 5 (5: 6: 7: 8: 9) times, K0 (2: 2: 1: 0: 1), P0 (1: 0: 0: 0: 0).
111 (117: 123: 129: 135: 145) sts.
Change to 3¾mm (US 5) needles.
Now work in patt, placing diamond panels as follows:
Row 1 (RS): P18 (21: 24: 27: 30: 35), *P2, Tw2R, Tw2L, work next 17 sts as row 1 of diamond panel, Tw2R, Tw2L, P2*, P1, (K1, P1) 8 times, rep from * to * once more, P18 (21: 24: 27: 30: 35).
Row 2: K2 (1: 0: 3: 2: 3), (inc2, P3tog) 4 (5: 6: 6: 7: 8) times, *K2, P4, work next 17 sts as row 2 of diamond panel, P4, K2*, P1, (K1, P1) 8 times, rep from * to * once more, (P3tog, inc2) 4 (5: 6: 6: 7: 8) times, K2 (1: 0: 3: 2: 3).
Row 3: P18 (21: 24: 27: 30: 35), *P2, Tw2L, Tw2R, work next 17 sts as row 3 of diamond panel, Tw2L, Tw2R, P2*, P1, (K1, P1) 8 times, rep from * to * once more, P18 (21: 24: 27: 30: 35).
Row 4: K2 (1: 0: 3: 2: 3), (P3tog, inc2) 4 (5: 6: 6: 7: 8) times, *K2, P4, work next 17 sts as row 4 of diamond panel, P4, K2*, P1, (K1, P1) 8 times, rep from * to * once more, (inc2, P3tog) 4 (5: 6: 6: 7: 8) times, K2 (1: 0: 3: 2: 3).
These 4 rows set the sts – 2 diamond panels with twist st braids either side, moss st at centre and side seam sts in blackberry st. Keeping patts correct as now set and repeating the 24 row diamond panel repeat throughout, cont as follows:
Cont straight until back measures 42 (42: 43: 43: 43: 43) cm, ending with a WS row.

Shape armholes
Keeping patt correct, cast off 5 (5: 6: 6: 7: 7) sts at beg of next 2 rows.
101 (107: 111: 117: 121: 131) sts.
Dec 1 st at each end of next 3 (5: 5: 7: 7: 9) rows, then on foll 4 (4: 5: 5: 5: 7) alt rows, then on foll 4th row. 85 (87: 89: 91: 95: 97) sts.
Cont straight until armhole measures 19 (20: 20: 21: 22: 23) cm, ending with a WS row.

Shape shoulders and back neck
Keeping patt correct, cast off 9 (9: 9: 9: 10: 10) sts at beg of next 2 rows. 67 (69: 71: 73: 75: 77) sts.
Next row (RS): Cast off 9 (9: 9: 9: 10: 10) sts, patt until there are 12 (12: 13: 13: 13: 14) sts on right needle and turn, leaving rem sts on a holder. Work each side of neck separately.
Cast off 4 sts at beg of next row.
Cast off rem 8 (8: 9: 9: 9: 10) sts.
With RS facing, rejoin yarn and cast off centre 25 (27: 27: 29: 29: 29) sts, patt to end.
Complete to match first side, rev shapings.

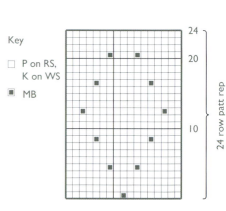

Key
☐ P on RS, K on WS
■ MB

24 row patt rep

LALA

LEFT FRONT

Cast on 66 (69: 72: 75: 78: 83) sts using 3mm (US 2/3) needles.

Row 1 (RS): K0 (1: 0: 0: 0: 0), P0 (2: 2: 1: 0: 1), (K2, P2) 5 (5: 6: 7: 8: 9) times, Tw2R, Tw2L, P2, (K2, P2) 4 times, Tw2R, Tw2L, (P2, K2) 3 times, K8.

Row 2: K8, (P2, K2) 3 times, P4, K2, (P2, K2) 4 times, P4, (K2, P2) 5 (5: 6: 7: 8: 9) times, K0 (2: 2: 1: 0: 1), P0 (1: 0: 0: 0: 0).

Row 3: K0 (1: 0: 0: 0: 0), P0 (2: 2: 1: 0: 1), (K2, P2) 5 (5: 6: 7: 8: 9) times, Tw2L, Tw2R, P2, (K2, P2) 4 times, Tw2L, Tw2R, (P2, K2) 3 times, K8.

Row 4: As row 2.

Last 4 rows form fancy rib with front opening edge 8 sts in g st.

Work in fancy rib for a further 15 rows, ending with a **RS** row.

Row 20 (WS): K8, (P2, K2tog) twice, P2, K2, P4, (K2, P2) twice, K2tog, (P2, K2) twice, P4, (K2, P2) 5 (5: 6: 7: 8: 9) times, K0 (2: 2: 1: 0: 1), P0 (1: 0: 0: 0: 0). 63 (66: 69: 72: 75: 80) sts.

Change to 3¾mm (US 5) needles.

Now work in patt, placing diamond panel as follows:

Row 1 (RS): P18 (21: 24: 27: 30: 35), P2, Tw2R, Tw2L, work next 17 sts as row 1 of diamond panel, Tw2R, Tw2L, P2, (K1, P1) 4 times, K8.

Row 2: K8, (P1, K1) 4 times, K2, P4, work next 17 sts as row 2 of diamond panel, P4, K2, (P3tog, inc2) 4 (5: 6: 6: 7: 8) times, K2 (1: 0: 3: 2: 3).

Row 3: P18 (21: 24: 27: 30: 35), P2, Tw2L, Tw2R, work next 17 sts as row 3 of diamond panel, Tw2L, Tw2R, P2, (K1, P1) 4 times, K8.

Row 4: K8, (P1, K1) 4 times, K2, P4, work next 17 sts as row 4 of diamond panel, P4, K2, (inc2, P3tog) 4 (5: 6: 6: 7: 8) times, K2 (1: 0: 3: 2: 3).

These 4 rows set the sts – diamond panel with twist st braids either side, front opening edge 8 sts in g st, moss st between this g st and twist st braid, and side seam sts in blackberry st.

Keeping patts correct as now set and repeating the 24 row diamond panel repeat throughout, cont as follows:

Cont straight until 20 rows less have been worked than on back to start of armhole shaping, ending with a WS row.

Shape front slope

Next row (RS): Patt to last 9 sts, K2tog, K7.

Working all front slope decreases as set by last row, cont as follows:

Keeping patt correct, dec 1 st at front slope edge on 4th and 3 foll 4th rows. 58 (61: 64: 67: 70: 75) sts.

Work 3 rows, ending with a WS row.

Shape armhole

Keeping patt correct, cast off 5 (5: 6: 6: 7: 7) sts at beg and dec 1 st at end of next row. 52 (55: 57: 60: 62: 67) sts.

Work 1 row.

Dec 1 st at armhole edge of next 3 (5: 5: 7: 7: 9) rows, then on foll 4 (4: 5: 5: 5: 7) alt rows, then on foll 4th row **and at same time** dec 1 st at front slope edge of 3rd and 3 (3: 4: 4: 4: 5) foll 4th rows. 40 (41: 41: 42: 44: 44) sts.

Dec 1 st at front slope edge **only** on 4th (2nd: 4th: 2nd: 2nd: 2nd) and 1 (3: 2: 3: 2: 0) foll 4th rows, then on 4 (3: 3: 3: 4: 5) foll 6th rows. 34 (34: 35: 35: 37: 38) sts.

Cont straight until left front matches back to start of shoulder shaping, ending with a WS row.

Shape shoulder

Keeping patt correct, cast off 9 (9: 9: 9: 10: 10) sts at beg of next and foll alt row, then 8 (8: 9: 9: 9: 10) sts at beg of foll alt row. 8 sts.

Inc 1 st at end of next row. 9 sts.

Cont in g st on these 9 sts only (for back neck border extension) until this strip measures 7 (7.5: 7.5: 8: 8: 8) cm, end with a WS row.

Cast off.

Mark positions for 6 buttons along left front opening edge – first button to come level with row 5, last button to come 2 cm below start of front slope shaping, and rem 4 buttons evenly spaced between.

RIGHT FRONT

Cast on 66 (69: 72: 75: 78: 83) sts using 3mm (US 2/3) needles.

Row 1 (RS): K8, (K2, P2) 3 times, Tw2R, Tw2L, P2, (K2, P2) 4 times, Tw2R, Tw2L, (P2, K2) 5 (5: 6: 7: 8: 9) times, P0 (2: 2: 1: 0: 1), K0 (1: 0: 0: 0: 0).

Row 2: P0 (1: 0: 0: 0: 0), K0 (2: 2: 1: 0: 1), (P2, K2) 5 (5: 6: 7: 8: 9) times, P4, K2, (P2, K2) 4 times, P4, (K2, P2) 3 times, K8.

Row 3: K8, (K2, P2) 3 times, Tw2L, Tw2R, P2, (K2, P2) 4 times, Tw2L, Tw2R, (P2, K2) 5 (5: 6: 7: 8: 9) times, P0 (2: 2: 1: 0: 1), K0 (1: 0: 0: 0: 0).

Row 4: As row 2.

Last 4 rows form fancy rib with front opening edge 8 sts in g st.

Row 5 (RS): K2, K2tog tbl, (yfwd) twice, K2tog (to make a buttonhole – on next row work twice into double yfwd), K2, rib to end.

Working a further 5 buttonholes in this way to correspond with positions marked for buttons on left front and noting that no further reference will be made to buttonholes, cont as follows:

Work in fancy rib for a further 14 rows, ending with a **RS** row.

Row 20 (WS): P0 (1: 0: 0: 0: 0), K0 (2: 2: 1: 0: 1), (P2, K2) 5 (5: 6: 7: 8: 9) times, P4, (K2, P2) twice, K2tog, (P2, K2) twice, P4, K2, P2, (K2tog, P2) twice, K8. 63 (66: 69: 72: 75: 80) sts.

Change to 3¾mm (US 5) needles.

Now work in patt, placing diamond panel as follows:

Row 1 (RS): K8, (P1, K1) 4 times, P2, Tw2R, Tw2L, work next 17 sts as row 1 of diamond panel, Tw2R, Tw2L, P2, P18 (21: 24: 27: 30: 35).

Row 2: K2 (1: 0: 3: 2: 3), (inc2, P3tog) 4 (5: 6: 6: 7: 8) times, K2, P4, work next 17 sts as row 2 of diamond panel, P4, K2, (K1, P1) 4 times, K8.

Row 3: K8, (P1, K1) 4 times, P2, Tw2L, Tw2R, work next 17 sts as row 3 of diamond panel, Tw2L, Tw2R, P2, P18 (21: 24: 27: 30: 35).

Row 4: K2 (1: 0: 3: 2: 3), (P3tog, inc2) 4 (5: 6: 6: 7: 8) times, K2, P4, work next 17 sts as row 4 of diamond panel, P4, K2, (K1, P1) 4 times, K8.

These 4 rows set the sts – diamond panel with twist st braids either side, front opening edge 8 sts in g st, moss st between this g st and twist st braid, and side seam sts in blackberry st.

LALA

Keeping patts correct as now set and repeating the 24 row diamond panel repeat throughout, cont as follows:
Cont straight until 20 rows less have been worked than on back to start of armhole shaping, ending with a WS row.
Shape front slope
Next row (RS): K7, K2tog tbl, patt to end.
Working all front slope decreases as set by last row, complete to match left front, reversing shapings.

SLEEVES (both alike)
Cast on 64 (66: 68: 70: 74: 76) sts using 3mm (US 2/3) needles.
Row 1 (RS): K1 (0: 0: 0: 0: 0), P2 (0: 1: 2: 0: 1), (K2, P2) 3 (4: 4: 4: 5: 5) times, (Tw2R, Tw2L, P2, K2, P2) 3 times, Tw2R, Tw2L, (P2, K2) 3 (4: 4: 4: 5: 5) times, P2 (0: 1: 2: 0: 1), K1 (0: 0: 0: 0: 0).
Row 2: P1 (0:0:0:0:0), K2 (0: 1: 2: 0: 1), (P2, K2) 3 (4: 4: 4: 5: 5) times, (P4, K2, P2, K2) 3 times, P4, (K2, P2) 3 (4: 4: 4: 5: 5) times, K2 (0: 1: 2: 0: 1), P1 (0: 0: 0: 0: 0).
Row 3: K1 (0:0:0:0:0), P2 (0: 1: 2: 0: 1), (K2, P2) 3 (4: 4: 4: 5: 5) times, (Tw2L, Tw2R, P2, K2, P2) 3 times, Tw2L, Tw2R, (P2, K2) 3 (4: 4: 4: 5: 5) times, P2 (0: 1: 2: 0: 1), K1 (0: 0: 0: 0: 0).
Row 4: As row 2.
Last 4 rows form fancy rib.
Work in fancy rib for a further 15 rows, ending with a **RS** row.
Row 20 (WS): P1 (0: 0: 0: 0: 0), K2 (0: 1: 2: 0: 1), (P2, K2) 3 (4: 4: 4: 5: 5) times, P4, K2, P2tog, K2, P4, K2, place marker on needle, P1, M1, P1, place marker on needle, K2, P4, K2, P2tog, K2, P4, (K2, P2) 3 (4: 4: 4: 5: 5) times, K2 (0: 1: 2: 0: 1), P1 (0: 0: 0: 0: 0). 63 (65: 67: 69: 73: 75) sts.
Change to 3¾mm (US 5) needles.
Now work in patt as follows:
Row 1 (RS): P13 (14: 15: 16: 18: 19), *P2, Tw2R, Tw2L, P5, Tw2R, Tw2L, P2*, slip marker onto right needle, yrn (to inc a st), P1, K1, P1, yrn (to inc a st), slip marker onto right needle, rep from * to * once more, P13 (14: 15: 16: 18: 19). 65 (67: 69: 71: 75: 77) sts.
Row 2: K1 (2: 3: 4: 2: 3), (inc2, P3tog) 3 (3: 3: 3: 4: 4) times, *K2, P4, K2, work row 1 of MB, K2, P4, K2*, slip marker onto right needle, K1, (P1, K1) twice, slip marker onto right needle, rep from * to * once more, (P3tog, inc2) 3 (3: 3: 3: 4: 4) times, K1 (2: 3: 4: 2: 3).
Row 3: P13 (14: 15: 16: 18: 19), *P2, Tw2L, Tw2R, P2, work row 2 of MB, P2, Tw2L, Tw2R, P2*, slip marker onto right needle, P1, (K1, P1) twice, slip marker onto right needle, rep from * to * once more, P13 (14: 15: 16: 18: 19).
Row 4: K1 (2: 3: 4: 2: 3), (P3tog, inc2) 3 (3: 3: 3: 4: 4) times, *K2, P4, K2, work row 3 of MB, K2, P4, K2*, slip marker onto right needle, P1, (K1, P1) twice, slip marker onto right needle, rep from * to * once more, (inc2, P3tog) 3 (3: 3: 3: 4: 4) times, K1 (2: 3: 4: 2: 3).
These 4 rows form patt – side sts in blackberry st, 2 panels of 2 twist st braids with bobbles between, and centre sts in double moss st.
Keeping patts correct as now set and repeating the 24 row diamond panel repeat throughout, cont as follows:
Work 6 rows, ending with a WS row.
Next row (RS): Patt to marker, slip marker onto right needle, yrn (to inc a st), patt to next marker, yrn (to inc a st), slip marker onto right needle, patt to end.
Working all sleeve increases as set by last row (by inc 1 st next to each marker), inc 1 st at each marker on 8th and 9 foll 8th rows, taking inc sts into double moss st - 27 sts now in double moss st at centre of rows. 87 (89: 91: 93: 97: 99) sts.
Cont straight until sleeve measures 47 (48: 49: 50: 51: 52) cm, ending with a WS row.
Shape top
Keeping patt correct, cast off 5 (5: 6: 6: 7: 7) sts at beg of next 2 rows.
77 (79: 79: 81: 83: 85) sts.
Dec 1 st at each end of next 3 rows, then on every foll alt row until 59 sts rem, then on foll 9 rows, ending with a WS row.
Cast off rem 41 sts.

MAKING UP
Press all pieces with a warm iron over a damp cloth.
Join both shoulder seams using back stitch or mattress stitch if preferred. Join cast-off ends of back neck border extensions, then sew one edge to back neck. Join side seams. Join sleeve seams. Insert sleeves into armholes. Sew on buttons.

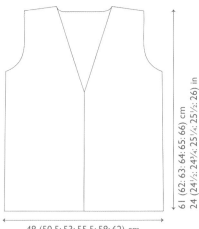

48 (50.5: 53: 55.5: 58: 62) cm
19 (20: 21: 22: 23: 24½) in

61 (62: 63: 64: 65: 66) cm
24 (24½: 24¾: 25¼: 25½: 26) in

47 (48: 49: 50: 51: 52) cm
18½ (19: 19¼: 19¾: 20: 20½) in

SWIRL ••
picture on pages 35 & 37

THE PATTERN

	XS	S	M	L	XL	XXL	
To fit bust	81	86	91	97	102	109	cm
	32	34	36	38	40	43	in

ROWAN HANDKNIT COTTON and **SUMMERLITE 4 ply** / Slate and Still Grey
Handknit Cotton
  5 5 5 6 6 7 x 50gm
Summerlite 4 ply
  2 3 3 3 4 4 x 50gm

NEEDLES
1 pair 6mm (no 4) (US 10) needles

TENSION
15 sts and 22 rows to 10 cm measured over double moss stitch using 6mm (US 10) needles and one strand each of Handknit Cotton and Summerlite 4 ply held together.

BACK
Cast on 63 (67: 71: 75: 79: 85) sts using 6mm (US 10) needles and one strand each of Handknit Cotton and Summerlite 4 ply held together.
Row 1 (RS): K1, *P1, K1, rep from * to end.
Row 2: (K1, P1) twice, K3, *P1, K1, rep from * to last 8 sts, P1, K3, (P1, K1) twice.
Row 3: (K1, P1) 3 times, P1, *K1, P1, rep from * to last 6 sts, (P1, K1) 3 times.
Row 4: (K1, P1) twice, K2, P1, *K1, P1, rep from * to last 6 sts, K2, (P1, K1) twice.
Last 4 rows set the sts – 5 sts in moss st at each end of row, central sts in double moss st and one st in rev st st between the 2 types of moss st.
Cont as now set until back measures 18 cm, ending after patt row 4 and a WS row. (For front, work 12 rows less here, so that front is 5.5 cm shorter than back.)
Place markers at both ends of last row (to denote top of side seam openings).
Now working **all** sts in double moss st, cont as follows:
Inc 1 st at each end of next row.
65 (69: 73: 77: 81: 87) sts.
Cont straight until back measures 20 (20: 21: 21: 21: 21) cm **from markers**, ending with a WS row.
Shape armholes
Place markers at both ends of last row (to denote base of armhole openings).
Next row (RS): K2, work 3 tog, patt to last 5 sts, work 3 tog, K2.
Next row: K2, patt to last 2 sts, K2.
Rep last row twice more, ending with a WS row. Last 4 rows set the sts and the decreases – 2 sts in g st at each end of rows and **double** decreases worked next to g st.
Keeping sts correct and working all decreases as now set, dec 2 sts at each end of next row.
57 (61: 65: 69: 73: 79) sts.
Work 1 row, ending with a WS row.
Divide for neck
Next row (RS): K2, patt 24 (26: 28: 30: 32: 35) sts, K1, K2tog and turn, leaving rem sts on a holder. 28 (30: 32: 34: 36: 39) sts.
Work each side of neck separately.

Next row (WS): K2, patt to last 2 sts, K2.
Last 2 rows set 2 sts in g st along neck edge.
Keeping sts correct as now set and working all neck decreases in same way as armhole decreases, dec 2 sts at neck edge of 3rd and 4 (4: 6: 5: 5: 4) foll 4th rows, then on 1 (0: 0: 1: 0: 1) foll 6th row, then on 1 (2: 1: 1: 2: 2) foll 8th rows **and at same time** dec 2 sts at armhole edge of next and 0 (1: 1: 3: 4: 4) foll 4th rows, then on 2 (2: 2: 1: 1: 2) foll 8th rows. 8 (8: 8: 8: 8: 9) sts.
Work 11 rows, ending with a WS row.
Cast off.
With RS facing, rejoin yarn to rem sts, K2, patt to last 2 sts, K2. 28 (30: 32: 34: 36: 39) sts.
Complete to match first side, reversing shapings.

FRONT
Work as given for back, noting the bracketed exception (so that front is 12 rows shorter than back).

MAKING UP
Press all pieces with a warm iron over a damp cloth.
Join shoulder seams using back stitch or mattress stitch if preferred. Join side seams between markers, noting that front side seam openings will be 12 rows shorter than on back.

43.5 (46: 48.5: 51: 53.5: 56: 60) cm
17 (18: 19: 20: 21: 22: 23½) in

61 (62: 63: 64: 65: 66) cm
24 (24½: 24¾: 25¼: 25½: 26) in

AYA
picture on page 24

THE PATTERN

	XS	S	M	L	XL	XXL	
To fit bust	81	86	91	97	102	109	cm
	32	34	36	38	40	43	in

ROWAN HANDKNIT COTTON / Feather

12 13 14 15 16 17 x 50gm

NEEDLES

1 pair 2¾mm (no 12) (US 2) needles
1 pair 3mm (no 11) (US 2/3) needles
1 pair 3¾mm (no 9) (US 5) needles

TENSION

24 sts and 30 rows to 10 cm measured over blackberry stitch using 3¾mm (US 5) needles.

SPECIAL ABBREVIATIONS

inc2 = make 3 sts from 1 st by working (K1, P1, K1) all into next st; **MB** = make bobble over next 3 rows – see below for details; **Tw2L** = K into back of second st on left needle, then K first st and slip both sts off left needle together; **Tw2R** = K into front of second st on left needle, then K first st and slip both sts off left needle together.

Bobble note: Bobbles are worked over 3 rows as follows:
Row 1 (WS): (P1, K1, P1, K1, P1) all into next st.
Row 2: P5.
Row 3: Slip 2 sts, P3tog, pass 2 slipped sts over.

BACK

Cast on 89 (95: 101: 104: 110: 119) sts using 2¾mm (US 2) needles.
Work in g st for 7 rows, end with a **RS** row.
Row 8 (WS): P2, *K1, yfrn, P2, rep from * to end. 118 (126: 134: 138: 146: 158) sts.
Row 9: K2, *P2, K2, rep from * to end.
Row 10: P2, *K2, P2, rep from * to end.
Last 2 rows form rib.
Work in rib for a further 11 rows, ending with a **RS** row.
Row 22 (WS): P2, *K2tog, P2, rep from * to end. 89 (95: 101: 104: 110: 119) sts.
Work in g st for 7 rows, ending with a **RS** row.
Change to 3¾mm (US 5) needles.
Row 30 (WS): K1 (0: 1: 1: 0: 0), (P1, K1) 4 (6: 7: 8: 10: 12) times, *K2, P1, M1P, P2, K11, P1, M1P, P2, K2*, K4 (4: 4: 2: 2: 4), M1, **K7 (7: 7: 6: 6: 7), M1, rep from ** 2 (2: 2: 3: 3: 2) times more, K4 (4: 4: 2: 2: 4), rep from * to * once more, (K1, P1) 4 (6: 7: 8: 10: 12) times, K1 (0: 1: 1: 0: 0). 97 (103: 109: 113: 119: 127) sts.
Now work in patt, placing diamond panels as follows:
Row 1 (RS): K1 (0: 1: 1: 0: 0), (P1, K1) 4 (6: 7: 8: 10: 12) times, *P2, Tw2R, Tw2L, work next 11 sts as row 1 of diamond panel, Tw2R, Tw2L, P2*, P33, rep from * to * once more, (K1, P1) 4 (6: 7: 8: 10: 12) times, K1 (0: 1: 1: 0: 0).
Row 2: K1 (0: 1: 1: 0: 0), (P1, K1) 4 (6: 7: 8: 10: 12) times, *K2, P4, work next 11 sts as row 2 of diamond panel, P4, K2*, inc2, (P3tog, inc2) 8 times, rep from * to * once more, (K1, P1) 4 (6: 7: 8: 10: 12) times, K1 (0: 1: 1: 0: 0).
Row 3: K1 (0: 1: 1: 0: 0), (P1, K1) 4 (6: 7: 8: 10: 12) times, *P2, Tw2R, Tw2L, work next 11 sts as row 3 of diamond panel, Tw2R, Tw2L, P2*, P35, rep from * to * once more, (K1, P1) 4 (6: 7: 8: 10: 12) times, K1 (0: 1: 1: 0: 0).
Row 4: K1 (0: 1: 1: 0: 0), (P1, K1) 4 (6: 7: 8: 10: 12) times, *K2, P4, work next 11 sts as row 4 of diamond panel, P4, K2*, P3tog, (inc2, P3tog) 8 times, rep from * to * once more, (K1, P1) 4 (6: 7: 8: 10: 12) times, K1 (0: 1: 1: 0: 0).
These 4 rows set the sts – 2 diamond panels with twist st braids either side, moss st at side seam edges and central sts in blackberry st.

(**Note:** The number of sts varies whilst working patt for central blackberry st panel. Count sts after patt rows 1 and 4 **only**. All st counts given presume there are 33 sts in central panel **at all times**.)
Keeping patts correct as now set and repeating the 24 row diamond panel repeat throughout, cont as follows:
Inc 1 st at each end of 5th and 3 foll 10th rows, taking inc sts into moss st.
105 (111: 117: 121: 127: 135) sts.
Cont straight until back measures 27 (27: 28: 28: 28: 28) cm, end with a WS row.
Shape armholes
Keeping patt correct, cast off 4 (4: 5: 5: 6: 6) sts at beg of next 2 rows.
97 (103: 107: 111: 115: 123) sts.
Dec 1 st at each end of next 3 (5: 5: 7: 7: 9) rows, then on foll 2 (2: 3: 2: 3: 3) alt rows, then on foll 4th row. 85 (87: 89: 91: 93: 97) sts.
Cont straight until armhole measures 19 (20: 20: 21: 22: 23) cm, ending with a WS row.
Shape shoulders and back neck
Keeping patt correct, cast off 7 (7: 7: 7: 8: 8) sts at beg of next 2 rows. 71 (73: 75: 77: 77: 81) sts.
Next row (RS): Cast off 7 (7: 7: 7: 8: 8) sts, patt until there are 11 (11: 12: 12: 11: 13) sts on right needle and turn, leaving rem sts on a holder.
Work each side of neck separately.
Cast off 4 sts at beg of next row.
Cast off rem 7 (7: 8: 8: 7: 9) sts.

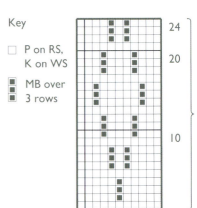

Key

☐ P on RS, K on WS

■ MB over 3 rows

24 row patt rep

AYA

With RS facing, rejoin yarn and cast off central sts until 17 (17: 18: 18: 18: 20) sts rem on left needle (and there should be one st on right needle), patt to end. 18 (18: 19: 19: 19: 21) sts. Complete to match first side, reversing shapings.

LEFT FRONT
Cast on 44 (47: 50: 53: 56: 59) sts using 2¾mm (US 2) needles.
Work in g st for 7 rows, ending with a **RS** row.
Row 8 (WS): K3, P2, *K1, yfrn, P2, rep from * to end. 57 (61: 65: 69: 73: 77) sts.
Row 9: *K2, P2, rep from * to last st, P1.
Row 10: K1, *K2, P2, rep from * to end.
Last 2 rows form rib.
Work in rib for a further 11 rows, ending with a **RS** row.
Row 22 (WS): K3, P2, *K2tog, P2, rep from * to end. 44 (47: 50: 53: 56: 59) sts.
Work in g st for 7 rows, ending with a **RS** row.
Change to 3¾mm (US 5) needles.
Row 30 (WS): K14 (14: 14: 17: 17: 14), (M1, K2) 1 (1: 1: 0: 0: 1) times, P2, M1P, P1, K11, P2, M1P, P1, K2, (K1, P1) 4 (6: 7: 8: 10: 12) times, K1 (0: 1: 1: 0: 0). 47 (50: 53: 55: 58: 62) sts.
Now work in patt, placing diamond panel as follows:
Row 1 (RS): K1 (0: 1: 1: 0: 0), (P1, K1) 4 (6: 7: 8: 10: 12) times, P2, Tw2R, Tw2L, work next 11 sts as row 1 of diamond panel, Tw2R, Tw2L, P17.
Row 2: K3, (P3tog, inc2) 3 times, K2, P4, work next 11 sts as row 2 of diamond panel, P4, K2, (K1, P1) 4 (6: 7: 8: 10: 12) times, K1 (0: 1: 1: 0: 0).
Row 3: K1 (0: 1: 1: 0: 0), (P1, K1) 4 (6: 7: 8: 10: 12) times, P2, Tw2R, Tw2L, work next 11 sts as row 3 of diamond panel, Tw2R, Tw2L, P17.
Row 4: K3, (inc2, P3tog) 3 times, K2, P4, work next 11 sts as row 4 of diamond panel, P4, K2, (K1, P1) 4 (6: 7: 8: 10: 12) times, K1 (0: 1: 1: 0: 0).
These 4 rows set the sts – diamond panel with twist st braids either side, moss st at side seam edge and front opening edge sts in blackberry st.

Keeping patts correct as now set and repeating the 24 row diamond panel repeat throughout, cont as follows:
Inc 1 st at beg of 5th and 3 foll 10th rows, taking inc sts into moss st. 51 (54: 57: 59: 62: 66) sts.
Cont straight until left front matches back to start of armhole shaping, ending with a WS row.

Shape armhole
Keeping patt correct, cast off 4 (4: 5: 5: 6: 6) sts at beg of next row. 47 (50: 52: 54: 56: 60) sts.
Work 1 row.
Dec 1 st at armhole edge of next 3 (5: 5: 7: 7: 9) rows, then on foll 2 (2: 3: 2: 3: 3) alt rows, then on foll 4th row. 41 (42: 43: 44: 45: 47) sts.
Cont straight until 22 (22: 22: 24: 24: 24) rows less have been worked than on back to start of shoulder shaping, ending with a WS row.

Shape front neck
Next row (RS): Patt 32 (32: 33: 34: 35: 37) sts, cast off rem 9 (10: 10: 10: 10: 10) sts.
Break yarn.
Rejoin yarn with **WS** facing and cont as follows:
Keeping patt correct, dec 1 st at neck edge of next 6 rows, then on foll 3 (3: 3: 4: 4: 4) alt rows, then on 2 foll 4th rows. 21 (21: 22: 22: 23: 25) sts.
Work 1 row, ending with a WS row.

Shape shoulder
Keeping patt correct, cast off 7 (7: 7: 7: 8: 8) sts at beg of next and foll alt row.
Work 1 row.
Cast off rem 7 (7: 8: 8: 7: 9) sts.

RIGHT FRONT
Cast on 44 (47: 50: 53: 56: 59) sts using 2¾mm (US 2) needles.
Work in g st for 7 rows, end with a **RS** row.
Row 8 (WS): *P2, K1, yfrn, rep from * to last 5 sts, P2, K3. 57 (61: 65: 69: 73: 77) sts.
Row 9: P1, *P2, K2, rep from * to end.
Row 10: *P2, K2, rep from * to last st, K1.
Last 2 rows form rib.
Work in rib for a further 11 rows, ending with a **RS** row.
Row 22 (WS): *P2, K2tog, rep from * to last 5 sts, P2, K3. 44 (47: 50: 53: 56: 59) sts.
Work in g st for 7 rows, ending with a **RS** row.
Change to 3¾mm (US 5) needles.
Row 30 (WS): K1 (0: 1: 1: 0: 0), (P1, K1) 4 (6: 7: 8: 10: 12) times, P2, M1P, P1, K11, P2, M1P, P1, K2, (K2, M1) 1 (1: 1: 0: 0: 1) times, K14 (14: 14: 17: 17: 14). 47 (50: 53: 55: 58: 62) sts.
Now work in patt, placing diamond panel as follows:
Row 1 (RS): P17, Tw2R, Tw2L, work next 11 sts as row 1 of diamond panel, Tw2R, Tw2L, P2, (K1, P1) 4 (6: 7: 8: 10: 12) times, K1 (0: 1: 1: 0: 0).
Row 2: K1 (0: 1: 1: 0: 0), (P1, K1) 4 (6: 7: 8: 10: 12) times, K2, P4, work next 11 sts as row 2 of diamond panel, P4, K2, (inc2, P3tog) 3 times, K3.
Row 3: P17, Tw2R, Tw2L, work next 11 sts as row 3 of diamond panel, Tw2R, Tw2L, P2, (K1, P1) 4 (6: 7: 8: 10: 12) times, K1 (0: 1: 1: 0: 0).
Row 4: K1 (0: 1: 1: 0: 0), (P1, K1) 4 (6: 7: 8: 10: 12) times, K2, P4, work next 11 sts as row 4 of diamond panel, P4, K2, (P3tog, inc2) 3 times, K3.
These 4 rows set the sts – diamond panel with twist st braids either side, moss st at side seam edge and front opening edge sts in blackberry st.
Keeping patts correct as now set and repeating the 24 row diamond panel repeat throughout, complete to match left front, reversing shapings and working first row of shape front neck as follows:

Shape front neck
Next row (RS): Cast off first 9 (10: 10: 10: 10: 10) sts, patt to end. 32 (32: 33: 34: 35: 37) sts.

SLEEVES (both alike)
Cast on 111 (111: 117: 123: 129: 129) sts using 2¾mm (US 2) needles.
Row 1 (RS): K3, *cast off next 3 sts (one st on right needle after cast-off), K2, rep from * to end. 57 (57: 60: 63: 66: 66) sts.
Work in g st for 6 rows, dec 1 st at end of last row and ending with a **RS** row. 56 (56: 59: 62: 65: 65) sts.
Row 8 (WS): P2, *K1, yfrn, P2, rep from * to end. 74 (74: 78: 82: 86: 86) sts.
Row 9: K2, *P2, K2, rep from * to end.

AYA

Row 10: P2, *K2, P2, rep from * to end.
Last 2 rows form rib.
Work in rib for a further 11 rows, ending with a **RS** row.
Row 22 (WS): P2, *K2tog, P2, rep from * to end. 56 (56: 59: 62: 65: 65) sts.
Work in g st for 7 rows, ending with a **RS** row.
Change to 3¾mm (US 5) needles.
Row 30 (WS): K11 (7: 8: 12: 13: 9), M1, K9 (7: 7: 11: 11: 9), (M1, K6) 0 (1: 1: 0: 0: 1) times, P1, M1P, P2, (K5, M1) 1 (1: 0: 1: 0: 0) times, K5 (5: 11: 5: 11: 11), P2, M1P, P1, (K6, M1) 0 (1: 1: 0: 0: 1) times, K9 (7: 7: 11: 11: 9), M1, K11 (7: 8: 12: 13: 9). 61 (63: 65: 67: 69: 71) sts.
Now work in patt as follows:
Row 1 (RS): Inc in first st, K0 (1: 0: 1: 0: 1), (P1, K1) 0 (0: 1: 1: 2: 2) times, P20, Tw2R, Tw2L, work next 11 sts as row 1 of diamond panel, Tw2R, Tw2L, P20, (K1, P1) 0 (0: 1: 1: 2: 2) times, K0 (1: 0: 1: 0: 1), inc in last st.
63 (65: 67: 69: 71: 73) sts.
Row 2: P0 (1: 0: 1: 0: 1), (K1, P1) 1 (1: 2: 2: 3: 3) times, K2, (inc2, P3tog) 4 times, K2, P4, work next 11 sts as row 2 of diamond panel, P4, K2, (P3tog, inc2) 4 times, K2, (P1, K1) 1 (1: 2: 2: 3: 3) times, P0 (1: 0: 1: 0: 1).
Row 3: P0 (1: 0: 1: 0: 1), (K1, P1) 1 (1: 2: 2: 3: 3) times, P20, Tw2R, Tw2L, work next 11 sts as row 3 of diamond panel, Tw2R, Tw2L, P20, (P1, K1) 1 (1: 2: 2: 3: 3) times, P0 (1: 0: 1: 0: 1).
Row 4: P0 (1: 0: 1: 0: 1), (K1, P1) 1 (1: 2: 2: 3: 3) times, K2, (P3tog, inc2) 4 times, K2, P4, work next 11 sts as row 4 of diamond panel, P4, K2, (inc2, P3tog) 4 times, K2, (P1, K1) 1 (1: 2: 2: 3: 3) times, P0 (1: 0: 1: 0: 1).
These 4 rows form patt – central diamond panel with twist st braids each side, side sts in moss st, and blackberry st between moss st and braids.
Keeping patts correct as now set and repeating the 24 row diamond panel repeat throughout, cont as follows:
Inc 1 st at each end of next (3rd: 3rd: 3rd: 3rd: 3rd) and every foll 6th row to 87 (87: 87: 85: 93: 91) sts, then on every foll - (8th: 8th: 8th: 8th: 8th) row until there are - (89: 91: 93: 97: 99) sts, taking inc sts into moss st.

Cont straight until sleeve measures 37 (38: 39: 40: 41: 42) cm, ending with a WS row.
Shape top
Keeping patt correct, cast off 4 (4: 5: 5: 6: 6) sts at beg of next 2 rows. 79 (81: 81: 83: 85: 87) sts.
Dec 1 st at each end of next and every foll alt row until 71 sts rem, then on foll 11 rows, ending with a WS row. 49 sts.
Cast off 3 sts at beg of next 6 rows.
Cast off rem 31 sts.

MAKING UP
Press all pieces with a warm iron over a damp cloth.
Join both shoulder seams using back stitch or mattress stitch if preferred.
Left front band
With RS facing and using 3mm (US 2/3) needles, pick up and knit 59 (62: 62: 65: 68: 68) sts down left front opening edge from neck shaping to top of hem border, and 15 sts down hem border to cast-on edge.
74 (77: 77: 80: 83: 83) sts.
Work in g st for 4 rows, ending with a **RS** row.
Row 5 (WS): K3, P2, *K1, yfrn, P2, rep from * to end. 97 (101: 101: 105: 109: 109) sts.
Row 6: *K2, P2, rep from * to last 5 sts, K5.
Row 7: K3, P2, *K2, P2, rep from * to end.
Last 2 rows form rib.
Cont in rib for a further 7 rows, ending with a **RS** row.
Cast off in rib (on **WS**).
Right front band
With RS facing and using 3mm (US 2/3) needles, pick up and knit 15 sts up hem border from cast-on edge to top of hem border, and 59 (62: 62: 65: 68: 68) sts up right front opening edge to neck shaping.
74 (77: 77: 80: 83: 83) sts.
Work in g st for 4 rows, ending with a **RS** row.
Row 5 (WS): P2, *K1, yfrn, P2, rep from * to last 3 sts, K3.
97 (101: 101: 105: 109: 109) sts.
Row 6: K5, *P2, K2, rep from * to end.
Row 7: *P2, K2, rep from * to last 5 sts, P2, K3.
Last 2 rows form rib.

Cont in rib for a further 7 rows, ending with a **RS** row.
Cast off in rib (on **WS**).
Neckband
With RS facing and using 3mm (US 2/3) needles, starting and ending at front opening edges, pick up and knit 9 sts from top of right front band, 9 (10: 10: 10: 10: 10) sts from front cast-off edge, 18 (18: 18: 20: 20: 20) sts up right side of front neck, 43 (45: 45: 47: 47: 47) sts from back, 18 (18: 18: 20: 20: 20) sts down left side of front neck, 9 (10: 10: 10: 10: 10) sts from front cast-off edge, and 9 sts from top of left front band.
115 (119: 119: 125: 125: 125) sts.
Work in g st for 6 rows, ending with a **RS** row.
Cast off knitwise (on **WS**).
Join side seams. Join sleeve seams. Insert sleeves into armholes.

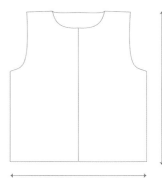

45.5 (48: 50.5: 53: 55.5: 59.5) cm
18 (19: 20: 21: 22: 23½) in

46 (47: 48: 49: 50: 51) cm
18 (18½: 19: 19¼: 19¾: 20) in

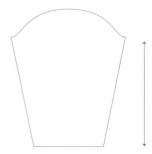

37 (38: 39: 40: 41: 42) cm
14½ (15: 15¼: 15¾: 16: 16½) in

FAIN ••
picture on pages 13 & 32

THE PATTERN

	XS	S	M	L	XL	XXL	
To fit bust	81	86	91	97	102	109	cm
	32	34	36	38	40	43	in

ROWAN CREATIVE LINEN / Silver
6 6 6 7 7 8 x 100gm

NEEDLES
1 pair 3¾mm (no 9) (US 5) needles
1 pair 4½mm (no 7) (US 7) needles
Cable needle

TENSION
Based on a stocking stitch tension of 20½ sts and 28 rows to 10 cm using 4½mm (US 7) needles.

SPECIAL ABBREVIATIONS
C6B = slip next 3 sts onto cable needle and leave at back of work, K3, then K3 from cable needle; **C6F** = slip next 3 sts onto cable needle and leave at front of work, K3, then K3 from cable needle.

ROUND NECK SWEATER

BACK
Cast on 152 (160: 168: 174: 178: 190) sts using 3¾mm (US 5) needles.
Row 1 (RS): K1 (1: 1: 0: 2: 0), P2, *K2, P2, rep from * to last 1 (1: 1: 0: 2: 0) sts, K1 (1: 1: 0: 2: 0).
Row 2: P1 (1: 1: 0: 2: 0), K2, *P2, K2, rep from * to last 1 (1: 1: 0: 2: 0) sts, P1 (1: 1: 0: 2: 0).
These 2 rows form rib.
Work in rib for a further 17 rows, ending with a **RS** row.
Row 20 (WS): (K2tog) 0 (0: 0: 1: 0: 1) times, P0 (0: 0: 1: 1: 1), (P1, K2tog, P1) 1 (2: 3: 3: 1: 2) times, (P1, K2tog, P2, K2, P2, K2tog, P1) 12 (12: 12: 12: 14: 14) times, (P1, K2tog, P1) 1 (2: 3: 3: 1: 2) times, P0 (0: 0: 1: 1: 1), (K2tog) 0 (0: 0: 1: 0: 1) times.
126 (132: 138: 142: 148: 156) sts.
Change to 4½mm (US 7) needles.
Now work in patt as follows:
Row 1 (RS): P3 (6: 9: 11: 4: 8), (P2, C6B, P2) 6 (6: 6: 6: 7: 7) times, (P2, C6F, P2) 6 (6: 6: 6: 7: 7) times, P3 (6: 9: 11: 4: 8).
Row 2: K3 (6: 9: 11: 4: 8), (K2, P6, K2) 12 (12: 12: 12: 14: 14) times, K3 (6: 9: 11: 4: 8).
Row 3: P3 (6: 9: 11: 4: 8), (P2, K6, P2) 12 (12: 12: 12: 14: 14) times, P3 (6: 9: 11: 4: 8).
Rows 4 to 9: As rows 2 and 3, 3 times.
Row 10: As row 2.
These 10 rows form patt.
Cont in patt for a further 54 rows, ending after patt row 4 and with a WS row.

Shape armholes
Keeping patt correct, cast off 3 sts at beg of next 2 rows. 120 (126: 132: 136: 142: 150) sts.**
Dec 1 st at each end of 3rd and foll 4th row. 116 (122: 128: 132: 138: 146) sts.
Work 45 (49: 49: 51: 55: 57) rows, ending with a WS row.

Shape back neck
Next row (RS): Patt 31 (33: 36: 37: 40: 44) sts and turn, leaving rem sts on a holder.
Work each side of neck separately.
Keeping patt correct, dec 1 st at neck edge of next 3 rows, ending with a WS row.
28 (30: 33: 34: 37: 41) sts.

Shape shoulder
Keeping patt correct, cast off 5 (5: 6: 6: 6: 7) sts at beg of next and foll 3 (2: 3: 3: 0: 1) alt rows, then – (6: –: –: 7: 8) sts at beg of foll – (1: –: –: 3: 2) alt rows **and at same time** dec 1 st at neck edge of next and foll 2 alt rows.
Work 1 row.
Cast off rem 5 (6: 6: 7: 7: 8) sts.
With RS facing, rejoin yarn to rem sts, cast off centre 54 (56: 56: 58: 58: 58) sts, patt to end.
Complete to match first side, rev shapings.

FRONT
Work as given for back.

SLEEVES (both alike)
Cast on 70 (72: 74: 78: 80: 82) sts using 3¾mm (US 5) needles.
Row 1 (RS): K0 (1: 2: 0: 1: 2), P2, *K2, P2, rep from * to last 0 (1: 2: 0: 1: 2) sts, K0 (1: 2: 0: 1: 2).
Row 2: P0 (1: 2: 0: 1: 2), K2, *P2, K2, rep from * to last 0 (1: 2: 0: 1: 2) sts, P0 (1: 2: 0: 1: 2).
These 2 rows form rib.
Work in rib for a further 17 rows, ending with a **RS** row.
Row 20 (WS): (K2tog, P2, K2) 1 (0: 0: 0: 0: 0) times, P2 (0: 0: 0: 1: 2), (K2tog) 1 (0: 0: 1: 1: 1) times, P1 (0: 1: 1: 1: 1), (P1, K2tog, P2, K2, P2, K2tog, P1) 4 (6: 6: 6: 6: 6) times, P1 (0: 1: 1: 1: 1), (K2tog) 1 (0: 0: 1: 1: 1) times, P2 (0: 0: 0: 1: 2), (K2, P2, K2tog) 1 (0: 0: 0: 0: 0) times.
58 (60: 62: 64: 66: 68) sts.
Change to 4½mm (US 7) needles.
Now work in patt as follows:
Row 1 (RS): (P1, C6B) 1 (0: 0: 0: 0: 0) times, K0 (0: 0: 0: 1: 2), P2 (0: 1: 2: 2: 2), (P2, C6B, P2) 2 (3: 3: 3: 3: 3) times, (P2, C6F, P2) 2 (3: 3: 3: 3: 3) times, P2 (0: 1: 2: 2: 2), K0 (0: 0: 0: 1: 2), (C6F, P1) 1 (0: 0: 0: 0: 0) times.
Row 2: K1 (0: 0: 0: 0: 0), P6 (0: 0: 0: 1: 2), K2 (0: 1: 2: 2: 2), (K2, P6, K2) 4 (6: 6: 6: 6: 6) times, K2 (0: 1: 2: 2: 2), P6 (0: 0: 0: 1: 2), K1 (0: 0: 0: 0: 0).
These 2 rows **set position** of patt as given for back.
Keeping patt correct as now set and as given for back, working cables on every 10th row, cont as follows:

FAIN

Inc 1 st at each end of next and every foll 4th row to 90 (96: 88: 94: 98: 104) sts, then on every foll 6th row until there are 100 (104: 104: 108: 112: 116) sts, taking inc sts into patt until there are 8 cables in total and rem sts into rev st st.
Cont straight until sleeve measures 45 (46: 47: 48: 49: 50) cm, ending with a WS row.

Shape top
Keeping patt correct, cast off 6 (7: 7: 7: 8: 8) sts at beg of next 4 (8: 8: 4: 8: 4) rows, then 7 (-: -: 8: -: 9) sts at beg of foll 4 (-: -: 4: -: 4) rows. Cast off rem 48 sts.

MAKING UP
Press all pieces with a warm iron over a damp cloth.
Join right shoulder seam using back stitch or mattress stitch if preferred.

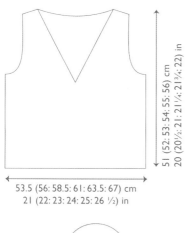

51 (52: 53: 54: 55: 56) cm
20 (20½: 21: 21¼: 21¾: 22) in

53.5 (56: 58.5: 61: 63.5: 67) cm
21 (22: 23: 24: 25: 26 ½) in

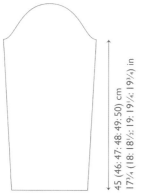

45 (46: 47: 48: 49: 50) cm
17¾ (18: 18½: 19: 19¼: 19¾) in

Neckband
With RS facing and using 3¾mm (US 5) needles, *pick up and knit 12 (11: 11: 10: 10: 10) sts down first side of neck, work across 54 (56: 56: 58: 58: 58) cast-off sts as follows: P0 (0: 0: 1: 1: 1), K5 (6: 6: 6: 6: 6) across top of cable, (P2 across top of 4 rev st st sts, K6 across top of cable) 4 times, P2 across top of 4 rev st st sts, K5 (6: 6: 6: 6: 6) across top of cable, P0 (0: 0: 1: 1: 1), pick up and 12 (11: 11: 10: 10: 10) sts up second side of neck, rep from * once more. 136 sts.
Row 1 (WS): P1, K2, *P2, K2, rep from * to last st, P1.
Row 2: K1, P2, *K2, P2, rep from * to last st, K1.
Rep last 2 rows 3 times more, ending with a **RS** row.
Cast off in rib (on **WS**).
Join left shoulder and neckband seam. Join side seams. Join sleeve seams. Insert sleeves into armholes.

V NECK SWEATER

BACK
Work as given for back of round neck sweater.

FRONT
Work as given for back of round neck sweater to **.
Work 4 rows, dec 1 st at each end of 3rd of these rows, ending after patt row 10 and with a WS row. 118 (124: 130: 134: 140: 148) sts.
Next row (RS): Patt 51 (54: 57: 59: 62: 66) sts, slip next 3 sts onto cable needle and leave at back of work, K3, then K2tog, K1, from cable needle, K4 and place marker at centre of these 4 sts, slip next 3 sts onto cable needle and leave at front of work, K1, K2tog, then K3 from cable needle, patt 51 (54: 57: 59: 62: 66) sts.
116 (122: 128: 132: 138: 146) sts.
Next row: Patt to within 7 sts of marker, P5, K4 (marker is at centre of these 4 sts), P5, patt to end.

Divide for front neck
Next row (RS): Work 2 tog, patt to within 8 sts of marker, K2tog, K6 and turn, leaving rem sts on a holder. 56 (59: 62: 64: 67: 71) sts. Work each side of neck separately.
Next row (WS): K2, P5, patt to end.
Next row: Patt to last 8 sts, K2tog, K6.
Last 2 rows set the sts and front neck decreases – neck edge has 2 sts in g st next to 5 sts in st st with all other sts still in patt. Keeping sts correct as now set and working all front slope decreases as set by last row, cont as follows:
Dec 1 st at neck edge of 2nd and foll 20 (20: 20: 21: 19: 18) alt rows, then on 1 (2: 2: 2: 4: 5) foll 4th rows. 33 (35: 38: 39: 42: 46) sts.
Work 1 row, ending with a WS row.

Shape shoulder
Cast off 5 (5: 6: 6: 6: 7) sts at beg of next and foll 4 (2: 4: 3: 0: 1) alt rows, then – (6: -: 7: 7: 8) sts at beg of foll – (2: -: 1: 4: 3) alt rows **and at same time** dec 1 st at front slope edge of 3rd row. 7 sts.
Work 1 row, ending with a WS row.
Cast off rem 7 sts.
With RS facing, rejoin yarn to rem sts and cont as follows:
Next row (RS): K6, K2tog tbl, patt to last 2 sts, work 2 tog. 56 (59: 62: 64: 67: 71) sts.
Next row (WS): Patt to last 7 sts, P5, K2.
Next row: K6, K2tog tbl, patt to end.
Last 2 rows set the sts and front neck decreases – neck edge has 2 sts in g st next to 5 sts in st st with all other sts still in patt. Keeping sts correct as now set and working all front slope decreases as set by last row, complete to match first side, reversing shapings.

SLEEVES (both alike)
Work as given for sleeves of round neck sweater.

MAKING UP
Press all pieces with a warm iron over a damp cloth.

Continued on next page …

QUIVER ••
picture on page 22

THE PATTERN

	XS	S	M	L	XL	XXL	
To fit bust	81	86	91	97	102	109	cm
	32	34	36	38	40	43	in

ROWAN SUMMERLITE 4 ply / Anchor Grey
3 3 3 4 4 5 x 50gm

NEEDLES
1 pair 2¾mm (no 12) (US 2) needles

TENSION
22 sts and 36 rows to 10 cm measured over pattern using 2¾mm (US 2) needles and **when lightly pressed**.

BACK and FRONT (both alike)
Cast on 87 (93: 99: 105: 109: 119) sts using 2¾mm (US 2) needles.
Work in g st for 6 rows, ending with a WS row.
Now work in patt as follows:
Row 1 (RS): Knit, wrapping yarn twice round needle for every st.
Row 2: Knit, dropping extra loops.
Rows 3 and 4: Knit.
Last 4 rows form patt.
Cont in patt until work measures 29 (29: 30: 30: 30: 30) cm, ending after patt row 2 and with a WS row.

Shape armholes
Place markers at both ends of last row (to denote base of armhole openings).
Next row (RS): K3, K3tog, K to last 6 sts, K3tog tbl, K3.
Keeping patt correct and working all armhole decreases as set by last row, cont as follows:
Dec 2 sts at each end of 4th and 1 (2: 3: 4: 4: 5) foll 4th rows, then on 2 (2: 2: 1: 2: 2) foll 8th rows. 67 (69: 71: 77: 77: 83) sts.
Work 7 (7: 3: 7: 3: 3) rows, ending with a WS row.

Shape neck
Next row (RS): (K3, K3tog) 1 (1: 0: 1: 0: 0) time, K20 (20: 27: 23: 29: 32) and turn, leaving rem sts on a holder. 24 (24: 27: 27: 29: 32) sts.
Work each side of neck separately.
Keeping patt correct and working all neck decreases in same way as armhole decreases, dec 2 sts at neck edge of 4th and 2 foll 4th rows, then on 2 foll 8th rows **and at same time** dec 2 sts at armhole edge of 8th (8th: 4th: 8th: 4th: 4th) and 0 (0: 1: 1: 2: 2) foll 8th rows, then on foll 12th row.
10 (10: 11: 11: 11: 14) sts.
Cont straight until armhole measures 24 (25: 25: 26: 27: 28) cm from markers, ending with a WS row.
Cast off.
With RS facing, rejoin yarn to rem sts, cast off centre 15 (17: 17: 19: 19: 19) sts, K to last 6 (6: 0: 6: 0: 0) sts, (K3tog tbl, K3) 1 (1: 0: 1: 0: 0) time. 24 (24: 27: 27: 29: 32) sts.
Complete to match first side, rev shapings.

MAKING UP
Gently easing pieces out to measurements given, press all pieces with a warm iron over a damp cloth.
Join shoulder seams using back stitch or mattress stitch if preferred. Join side seams.

53 (54: 55: 56: 57: 58) cm
21 (21¼: 21¾: 22: 22½: 23) in

39.5 (42: 44.5: 47: 49.5: 53.5) cm
15½ (16½: 17½: 18½: 19½: 21) in

FAIN - Continued from previous page.

Back neckband
With RS facing and using 3¾mm (US 5) needles, pick up and knit 13 (12: 12: 11: 11: 11) sts down first side of neck, work across 54 (56: 56: 58: 58: 58) cast-off sts as follows:
P0 (0: 0: 1: 1: 1), K5 (6: 6: 6: 6: 6) across top of cable, (P2 across top of 4 rev st st sts, K6 across top of cable) 4 times, P2 across top of 4 rev st st sts, K5 (6: 6: 6: 6: 6) across top of cable, P0 (0: 0: 1: 1: 1), then pick up and 13 (12: 12: 11: 11: 11) sts up second side of neck. 70 sts.
Row 1 (WS): P2, *K2, P2, rep from * to end.
Row 2: K2, *P2, K2, rep from * to end.
Rep last 2 rows 3 times more, ending with a **RS** row.
Cast off in rib (on **WS**).
Using back stitch or mattress stitch if preferred, join shoulder seams, attaching cast-off edges of last 7 sts of front neck slope to row-end edges of back neckband.
Join side seams. Join sleeve seams. Insert sleeves into armholes.

WAVER
picture on pages 12 & 14

THE PATTERN

	XS	S	M	L	XL	XXL
To fit bust	81	86	91	97	102	109 cm
	32	34	36	38	40	43 in

ROWAN CREATIVE LINEN / Silver

6 6 6 7 7 8 x 100gm

NEEDLES

1 pair 3¼mm (no 10) (US 3) needles
1 pair 4mm (no 8) (US 6) needles

TENSION

20 sts and 29 rows to 10 cm measured over pattern using 4mm (US 6) needles.

Pattern note: The st created by the "yfwd" made whilst working the patt will be dropped and unravelled later. Therefore this st is NOT included in any st count. All st counts given presume there are just TWO sts in this rib line **at all times**. When working shaping at the top of a rib line that has not yet had the corresponding st dropped, drop the relevant st and unravel it back to the "yfwd" BEFORE working the shaping.

BACK and FRONT (both alike)

Cast on 102 (106: 112: 116: 122: 132) sts using 4mm (US 6) needles.
Next row (WS): K6 (4: 7: 5: 8: 5), (K2, P2) 0 (1: 1: 0: 0: 0) times, *K1, yfwd – see pattern note, K1, P2, K2, P2, rep from * to last 8 (10: 13: 7: 10: 7) sts, K1, yfwd – see pattern note, K1, (P2, K2) 0 (1: 1: 0: 0: 0) times, K6 (4: 7: 5: 8: 5).
Now work in patt as follows:
Row 1 (RS): K6 (4: 7: 5: 8: 5), (P2, K2) 0 (1: 1: 0: 0: 0) times, *P3, K2, P2, K2, rep from * to last 9 (11: 14: 8: 11: 8) sts, P3, (K2, P2) 0 (1: 1: 0: 0: 0) times, K6 (4: 7: 5: 8: 5).
Row 2: K6 (4: 7: 5: 8: 5), (K2, P2) 0 (1: 1: 0: 0: 0) times, *K3, P2, K2, P2, rep from * to last 9 (11: 14: 8: 11: 8) sts, K3, (P2, K2) 0 (1: 1: 0: 0: 0) times, K6 (4: 7: 5: 8: 5).
Rows 3 and 4: As rows 1 and 2.
Row 5: As row 3.
Row 6: K6 (4: 7: 5: 8: 5), (K1, yfwd – see pattern note, K1, P2) 0 (1: 1: 0: 0: 0) times, *K1, drop next st and unravel back down to "yfwd" 6 rows below, K1, P2, K1, yfwd – see pattern note, K1, P2, rep from * to last 9 (11: 14: 8: 11: 8) sts, K1, drop next st and unravel back down to "yfwd" 6 rows below, K1, (P2, K1, yfwd – see pattern note, K1) 0 (1: 1: 0: 0: 0) times, K6 (4: 7: 5: 8: 5).
Row 7: K6 (4: 7: 5: 8: 5), (P3, K2) 0 (1: 1: 0: 0: 0) times, *P2, K2, P3, K2, rep from * to last 8 (11: 14: 7: 10: 7) sts, P2, (K2, P3) 0 (1: 1: 0: 0: 0) times, K6 (4: 7: 5: 8: 5).
Row 8: K6 (4: 7: 5: 8: 5), (K3, P2) 0 (1: 1: 0: 0: 0) times, *K2, P2, K3, P2, rep from * to last 8 (11: 14: 7: 10: 7) sts, K2, (P2, K3) 0 (1: 1: 0: 0: 0) times, K6 (4: 7: 5: 8: 5).
Rows 9 and 10: As rows 7 and 8.
Row 11: As row 7.
Row 12: K6 (4: 7: 5: 8: 5), (K1, drop next st and unravel back down to "yfwd" 6 rows below, K1, P2) 0 (1: 1: 0: 0: 0) times, * K1, yfwd – see pattern note, K1, P2, K1, drop next st and unravel back down to "yfwd" 6 rows below, K1, P2, rep from * to last 8 (11: 14: 7: 10: 7) sts, K1, yfwd – see pattern note, K1, (P2, K1, drop next st and unravel back down to "yfwd" 6 rows below, K1) 0 (1: 1: 0: 0: 0) times, K6 (4: 7: 5: 8: 5).

These 12 rows set the sts – edge 6 (4: 7: 5: 8: 5) sts in g st (for side seam opening borders) and all other sts in patt.
Cont as set for a further 24 rows, ending with a WS row.
Place markers at both ends of last row (to denote top of side seam openings).
Next row (RS): K6 (4: 7: 5: 8: 5), patt to last 6 (4: 7: 5: 8: 5) sts, K6 (4: 7: 5: 8: 5).
Next row: P6 (4: 7: 5: 8: 5), patt to last 6 (4: 7: 5: 8: 5) sts, P6 (4: 7: 5: 8: 5).
Last 2 rows set the sts – edge sts now in st st instead of g st.
Cont as now set until work measures 36 (36: 37: 37: 37: 37) cm, ending with a WS row.
Shape armholes
Keeping patt correct (see pattern note), cast off 4 (4: 5: 5: 6: 6) sts at beg of next 2 rows. 94 (98: 102: 106: 110: 120) sts.
Dec 1 st at each end of next 3 (5: 5: 7: 7: 9) rows, then on foll 4 (3: 4: 3: 4: 5) alt rows, then on foll 4th row.
78 (80: 82: 84: 86: 90) sts.
Cont straight until armhole measures 16 (17: 17: 18: 19: 20) cm, ending with a WS row.
Shape neck
Next row (RS): Patt 18 (18: 19: 19: 20: 22) sts (see pattern note) and turn, leaving rem sts on a holder.
Work each side of neck separately.
Keeping patt correct, cast off 3 sts at beg of next row. 15 (15: 16: 16: 17: 19) sts.
Dec 1 st at neck edge of next 3 rows, then on foll alt row.
11 (11: 12: 12: 13: 15) sts.
Work 1 row, ending with a WS row.
Shape shoulder
Cast off 5 (5: 5: 5: 6: 7) sts at beg (see pattern note) and dec 1 st at end of next row.
Work 1 row.
Cast off rem 5 (5: 6: 6: 6: 7) sts.
With RS facing, rejoin yarn to rem sts, cast off centre 42 (44: 44: 46: 46: 46) sts (see pattern note), patt to end.
Complete to match first side, reversing shapings.

Continued on next page …

NOVA
picture on page 27

THE PATTERN
ROWAN SUMMERLITE DK / Mocha
2 x 50gm

NEEDLES
1 pair 2¾mm (no 12) (US 2) needles
1 pair 3¼mm (no 10) (US 3) needles

TENSION
25 sts and 34 rows to 10 cm measured over pattern using 3¼mm (US 3) needles.

HAT
Cast on 154 sts using 2¾mm (US 2) needles.
Row 1 (RS): K2, *P2, K2, rep from * to end.
Row 2: P2, *K2, P2, rep from * to end.
These 2 rows form rib.
Cont in rib for a further 20 rows, ending with a WS row.
Change to 3¼mm (US 3) needles.
Now work in patt as follows:
Row 1 (RS): Purl.
Row 2: K1, *P3tog, (K1, P1, K1) all into next st, rep from * to last st, K1.
Row 3: Purl.
Row 4: K1, *(K1, P1, K1) all into next st, P3tog, rep from * to last st, K1.
These 4 rows form patt.
Cont in patt until hat measures 24 cm, ending after patt row 4 and with a WS row.
Shape top
Row 1 (RS): Purl.
Row 2: K1, *P3tog, K1, rep from * to last st, K1. 78 sts
Row 3: Purl.
Row 4: K1, *K2tog, rep from * to last st, K1. 40 sts.
Row 5: Purl.
Row 6: As row 4. 21 sts.
Row 7: P1, *P2tog, rep from * to end. 11 sts.
Break yarn and thread through rem 11 sts.
Pull up tight and fasten off securely.

MAKING UP
Do NOT press. Join back seam.

WAVER - Continued from previous page.

SLEEVES (both alike)
Cast on 54 (56: 58: 60: 62: 64) sts using 4mm (US 6) needles.
Next row (WS): K0 (0: 0: 0: 0: 1), P0 (0: 0: 1: 2: 2), K0 (1: 2: 2: 2: 2), *P2, K1, yfwd – see pattern note, K1, P2, K2, rep from * to last 6 (7: 0: 1: 2: 3) sts, P2 (2: 0: 1: 2: 2), (K1, yfwd – see pattern note) 1 (1: 0: 0: 0: 0) times, K1 (1: 0: 0: 0: 1), P2 (2: 0: 0: 0: 0), K0 (1: 0: 0: 0: 0).
This row **sets position** of patt as given for back and front.
Now working the 12 row patt repeat as given for back and front, inc and dec sts on 6th and every foll 6th row, cont as follows:
Work 10 rows, ending with a WS row.
Inc 1 st at each end of next and 10 (9: 7: 6: 10: 9) foll 10th rows, then on 1 (2: 4: 5: 2: 3) foll 12th rows, taking inc sts into rib until there are sufficient sts to take into patt.
78 (80: 82: 84: 88: 90) sts.
Cont straight until sleeve measures 47 (48: 49: 50: 51: 52) cm, ending with a WS row.
Shape top
Keeping patt correct (see pattern note), cast off 4 (4: 5: 5: 6: 6) sts at beg of next 2 rows. 70 (72: 72: 74: 76: 78) sts.
Dec 1 st at each end of next and every foll alt row until 56 sts rem, then on foll 7 rows, ending with a WS row.
Cast off rem 42 sts.

MAKING UP
Press all pieces with a warm iron over a damp cloth.
Join right shoulder seam using back stitch or mattress stitch if preferred.
Neckband
With RS facing and using 3¼mm (US 3) needles, pick up and knit 8 sts down left side of front neck, 42 (44: 44: 46: 46: 46) sts from front, 8 sts up right side of front neck, 8 sts down right side of back neck, 42 (44: 44: 46: 46: 46) sts from back, and 8 sts up left side of back neck. 116 (120: 120: 124: 124: 124) sts.
Beg with a K row, work in rev st st for 4 rows, ending with a **RS** row.
Cast off knitwise (on **WS**).
Join left shoulder and neckband seam. Join side seams, leaving side seams open below markers (for side seam openings). Join sleeve seams. Insert sleeves into armholes.

51 (53: 56: 58: 61: 66) cm
20 (21: 22: 23: 24: 26) in

55 (56: 57: 58: 59: 60) cm
21½ (22: 22½: 22¾: 23¼: 23¾) in

47 (48: 49: 50: 51: 52) cm
18½ (19: 19¼: 19¾: 20: 20½) in

EILA
picture on page 31

THE PATTERN

	XS	S	M	L	XL	XXL	
To fit bust	81	86	91	97	102	109	cm
	32	34	36	38	40	43	in

ROWAN SUMMERLITE DK / Silvery Blue and Seashell

Silvery Blue	6	6	6	7	7	8	x 50gm
Seashell	6	6	6	7	7	8	x 50gm

One-colour version

	11	12	12	13	14	15	x 50gm

NEEDLES
1 pair 4mm (no 8) (US 6) needles
1 pair 4½mm (no 7) (US 7) needles

TENSION
16 sts and 22 rows to 10 cm measured over pattern using 4½mm (US 7) needles and 2 strands of yarn held together.

Pattern note: When working patt from chart, every WS row is a K row. Where yarn has been wound round needle 2 or 3 times on previous RS row, drop these extra loops on the foll WS row.
To prevent side edges of knitting from becoming loose and uneven, replace any 'yarn over needle 3 times' at the beginning and ends of rows on chart with 'yarn over needle twice'.

BACK
Cast on 76 (82: 86: 90: 94: 102) sts using 4mm (US 6) needles and one strand of each colour of yarn held together.
Row 1 (RS): K1 (0: 2: 0: 2: 2), P2, *K2, P2, rep from * to last 1 (0: 2: 0: 2: 2) sts, K1 (0: 2: 0: 2: 2).
Row 2: P1 (0: 2: 0: 2: 2), K2, *P2, K2, rep from * to last 1 (0: 2: 0: 2: 2) sts, P1 (0: 2: 0: 2: 2).
These 2 rows form rib.
Cont in rib for a further 7 rows, ending with a **RS** row.
Row 10 (WS): P0 (0: 2: 0: 0: 2), (K2tog) 0 (1: 1: 0: 0: 1) times, P1 (2: 2: 0: 2: 2), *K2, P2, K2tog, P2, rep from * to last 3 (6: 0: 2: 4: 0) sts, K2 (2: 0: 2: 2: 0), P1 (2: 0: 0: 2: 0), (K2tog) 0 (1: 0: 0: 0: 0) times. 67 (71: 75: 79: 83: 89) sts.
Change to 4½mm (US 7) needles.
Work in g st for 6 rows, ending with a WS row.
Beg and ending rows as indicated and repeating the 36 row patt repeat throughout, now work in patt from chart for body (see pattern note) as follows:
Cont straight until back measures 23 (23: 24: 24: 24: 24) cm, ending with a WS row.
Shape armholes
Keeping patt correct, cast off 2 sts at beg of next 2 rows. 63 (67: 71: 75: 79: 85) sts.
Dec 1 st at each end of next 1 (1: 3: 3: 5: 5) rows, then on foll 1 (2: 1: 2: 1: 3) alt rows. 59 (61: 63: 65: 67: 69) sts.
Cont straight until armhole measures 16 (17: 17: 18: 19: 20) cm, ending with a WS row.
Shape back neck
Next row (RS): Patt 12 (12: 13: 13: 14: 15) sts and turn, leaving rem sts on a holder.
Work each side of neck separately.
Keeping patt correct, dec 1 st at neck edge of next 3 rows, ending with a WS row.
9 (9: 10: 10: 11: 12) sts.
Shape shoulder
Cast off 4 (4: 4: 4: 5: 5) sts at beg and dec 1 st at end of next row.
Work 1 row.
Cast off rem 4 (4: 5: 5: 5: 6) sts.
With RS facing, rejoin yarns to rem sts, cast off centre 35 (37: 37: 39: 39: 39) sts, patt to end.
Complete to match first side, reversing shapings.

FRONT
Work as given for back until 8 (8: 8: 10: 10: 10) rows less have been worked than on back to start of shoulder shaping, ending with a WS row.
Shape front neck
Next row (RS): Patt 14 (14: 15: 16: 17: 18) sts and turn, leaving rem sts on a holder.
Work each side of neck separately.
Keeping patt correct, dec 1 st at neck edge of next 4 rows, then on foll 1 (1: 1: 2: 2: 2) alt rows. 9 (9: 10: 10: 11: 12) sts.
Work 1 row, ending with a WS row.
Shape shoulder
Cast off 4 (4: 4: 4: 5: 5) sts at beg and dec 1 st at end of next row.
Work 1 row.
Cast off rem 4 (4: 5: 5: 5: 6) sts.
With RS facing, rejoin yarns to rem sts, cast off centre 31 (33: 33: 33: 33: 33) sts, patt to end.
Complete to match first side, rev shapings.

SLEEVES (both alike)
Cast on 40 (42: 44: 46: 46: 50) sts using 4mm (US 6) needles and one strand of each colour of yarn held together.
Row 1 (RS): K0 (0: 1: 0: 0: 0), P1 (2: 2: 0: 0: 2), *K2, P2, rep from * to last 3 (0: 1: 2: 2: 0) sts, K2 (0: 1: 2: 2: 0), P1 (0: 0: 0: 0: 0).
Row 2: P0 (0: 1: 0: 0: 0), K1 (2: 2: 0: 0: 2), *P2, K2, rep from * to last 3 (0: 1: 2: 2: 0) sts, P2 (0: 1: 2: 2: 0), K1 (0: 0: 0: 0: 0).
These 2 rows form rib.
Cont in rib for a further 7 rows, ending with a **RS** row.
Row 10 (WS): (K2tog) 0 (0: 0: 0: 0: 1) times, P0 (0: 1: 2: 2: 2), K1 (2: 2: 2: 2: 2), *P2, K2tog, P2, K2, rep from * to last 7 (0: 1: 2: 2: 4) sts, P2 (0: 1: 2: 2: 2), (K2tog) 1 (0: 0: 0: 0: 1) times, P2 (0: 0: 0: 0: 0), K1 (0: 0: 0: 0: 0).
35 (37: 39: 41: 41: 43) sts.
Change to 4½mm (US 7) needles.
Work in g st for 6 rows, inc 1 st at each end of 3rd of these rows and ending with a WS row. 37 (39: 41: 43: 43: 45) sts.

EILA

Beg and ending rows as indicated and repeating the 36 row patt repeat throughout, now work in patt from chart for sleeve (see pattern note) as follows:
Inc 1 st at each end of 7th (7th: 9th: 9th: 9th: 9th) and every foll 10th (10th: 12th: 12th: 12th: 12th) row to 53 (53: 55: 53: 51: 51) sts, then on every foll – (12th: –: 14th: 14th: 14th) row until there are - (55: –: 57: 57: 59) sts, taking inc sts into patt.
Cont straight until sleeve measures 47 (48: 49: 50: 51: 52) cm, ending with a WS row.

Shape top
Keeping patt correct, cast off 2 sts at beg of next 2 rows. 49 (51: 51: 53: 53: 55) sts.
Dec 1 st at each end of next and every foll alt row until 37 sts rem, then on foll 7 rows, ending with a WS row.
Cast off rem 23 sts.

MAKING UP
Press all pieces with a warm iron over a damp cloth. Join right shoulder seam using back stitch or mattress stitch if preferred.

Neckband
With RS facing, using 4mm (US 6) needles and one strand of each colour of yarn held together, pick up and knit 9 (10: 10: 12: 12: 12) sts down left side of front neck, 31 (33: 33: 33: 33: 33) sts from front, 9 (10: 10: 12: 12: 12) sts up right side of front neck, 7 sts down right side of back neck, 34 (37: 37: 40: 40: 40) sts from back, and 7 sts up left side of back neck.
97 (104: 104: 111: 111: 111) sts.
Row 1 (WS): P2, K2, P2, *inc knitwise in next st, P2, K2, P2, rep from * to end.
110 (118: 118: 126: 126: 126) sts.
Row 2: K2, *P2, K2, rep from * to end.
Row 3: P2, *K2, P2, rep from * to end.
Rows 4 and 5: As rows 2 and 3.
Cast off in rib.
Join left shoulder and neckband seam.
Join side seams.
Join sleeve seams. Insert sleeves into armholes.

41.5 (44: 46.5: 49: 51.5: 55.5) cm
16½ (17½: 18½: 19¼: 20¼: 21¾) in

42 (43: 44: 45: 46: 47) cm
16½ (17: 17½: 17¾: 18: 18½) in

47 (48: 49: 50: 51: 52) cm
18½ (19: 19¼: 19¾: 20: 20½) in

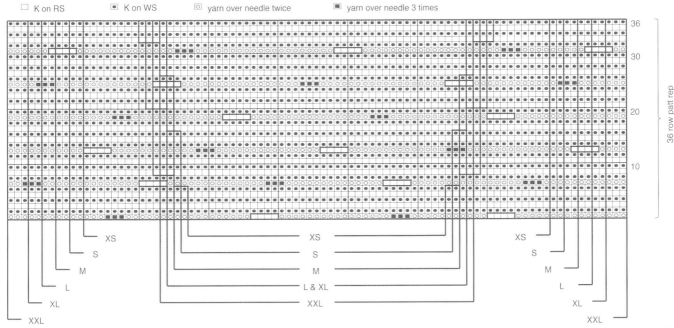

Key: □ K on RS ● K on WS ○ yarn over needle twice ■ yarn over needle 3 times

36 row patt rep

ARIA
picture on page 29

THE PATTERN

XS	S	M	L	XL	XXL	
To fit bust
81	**86**	**91**	**97**	**102**	**109**	**cm**
32	34	36	38	40	43	in

ROWAN CREATIVE LINEN / Silver
5 5 5 6 6 7 x 100gm

NEEDLES
1 pair 5mm (no 6) (US 8) needles

TENSION
18 sts and 24 rows to 10 cm measured over stocking stitch using 5mm (US 8) needles.

BACK
Cast on 74 (78: 82: 88: 92: 98) sts using 5mm (US 8) needles.
Row 1 (RS): K to last st, pick up loop lying between needles and place this loop on right needle (**Note**: this loop does **NOT** count as a st), with yarn at back (**WS**) of work slip last st **purlwise**.
Row 2: P tog the first st and the picked-up loop, P to last st, pick up loop lying between needles and place this loop on right needle (**Note**: this loop does **NOT** count as a st), with yarn at front (**WS**) of work slip last st **purlwise**.
Row 3: K tog tbl the first st and the picked-up loop, K to last st, pick up loop lying between needles and place this loop on right needle (**Note**: this loop does **NOT** count as a st), with yarn at back (**WS**) of work slip last st **purlwise**.
The last 2 rows set the sts – st st with a slip st edging.
Cont as set for a further 37 rows, ending with a WS row.
Place markers at both ends of last row (to denote top of side seam openings).
Beg with a K row, now work **all** sts in st st and cont as follows:
Work 72 (72: 74: 74: 74: 74) rows, ending with a WS row.
Shape armholes
Cast off 3 (3: 4: 4: 5: 5) sts at beg of next 2 rows. 68 (72: 74: 80: 82: 88) sts.
Dec 1 st at each end of next 1 (3: 3: 5: 5: 7) rows, then on foll 2 (1: 1: 1: 1: 1) alt rows, then on foll 4th row.
60 (62: 64: 66: 68: 70) sts.
Work 25 (27: 27: 27: 29: 31) rows, ending with a WS row.
Shape back neck
Next row (RS): K17 (17: 18: 18: 19: 20), pick up loop lying between needles and place this loop on right needle (**Note**: this loop does **NOT** count as a st), with yarn at back (**WS**) of work slip next st **purlwise** and turn, leaving rem sts on a holder.
18 (18: 19: 19: 20: 21) sts.
Work each side of neck separately.
Now working slip st edging along back neck edge, cont as follows:
Work 1 row, ending with a WS row.
Next row (RS): K to last 7 sts, K3tog tbl, patt rem 4 sts.
Working all back neck decreases as set by last row, dec 2 sts at neck edge of 2nd and foll alt row.
12 (12: 13: 13: 14: 15) sts.
Work 1 row, ending with a WS row.
Shape shoulder
Cast off 6 (6: 6: 6: 7: 7) sts at beg of next row.
Work 1 row.
Cast off rem 6 (6: 7: 7: 7: 8) sts.
With RS facing, rejoin yarn to rem sts, cast off centre 24 (26: 26: 28: 28: 28) sts, K to end.
Complete to match first side, reversing shapings.

LEFT FRONT
Cast on 63 (68: 72: 78: 82: 87) sts using 5mm (US 8) needles.
Beg with row 1 and a K row, work in st st with slip st edging as given for back for 40 rows, ending with a WS row.
Place marker at end of last row (to denote top of side seam opening).
Keeping slip st edging along front opening edge, now work all other sts in st st, beg with a K row, as follows:
Work 26 rows, ending with a WS row.
Shape front slope
Next row (RS): K to last 7 sts, K3tog tbl, patt rem 4 sts.
Working all front slope decreases as set by last row, cont as follows:
Dec 2 sts at front slope edge of 2nd and foll 4 (7: 8: 11: 12: 12) foll alt rows, then on 8 (7: 7: 5: 5: 5) foll 4th rows.
35 (36: 38: 42: 44: 49) sts.
Work 3 (1: 1: 3: 1: 1) rows, ending with a WS row.
Shape armhole
Cast off 3 (3: 4: 4: 5: 5) sts at beg and dec 2 (0: 0: 2: 0: 0) sts at end of next row.
30 (33: 34: 36: 39: 44) sts.
Work 1 row.

ARIA

Dec 1 st at armhole edge of next 1 (3: 3: 5: 5: 7) rows, then on foll 2 (1: 1: 1: 1: 1) alt rows, then on foll 4th row **and at same time** dec 2 sts at front slope edge on 3rd (next: next: 3rd: next: next) and 1 (2: 2: 2: 2: 3) foll 4th rows. 22 (22: 23: 23: 26: 27) sts.
Dec 2 sts at front slope edge **only** on 2nd (4th: 4th: 4th: 2nd: 4th) and 0 (0: 0: 0: 1: 1) foll 4th row, then on 4 foll 6th rows. 12 (12: 13: 13: 14: 15) sts.
Work 7 rows, ending with a WS row.
Shape shoulder
Cast off 6 (6: 6: 6: 7: 7) sts at beg of next row.
Work 1 row.
Cast off rem 6 (6: 7: 7: 7: 8) sts.

RIGHT FRONT
Cast on 63 (68: 72: 78: 82: 87) sts using 5mm (US 8) needles.
Beg with row 1 and a K row, work in st st with slip st edging as given for back for 40 rows, ending with a WS row.
Place marker at beg of last row (to denote top of side seam opening).
Keeping slip st edging along front opening edge, now work all other sts in st st, beg with a K row, as follows:
Work 26 rows, ending with a WS row.
Shape front slope
Next row (RS): Patt 4 sts, K3tog, K to end.
Working all front slope decreases as set by last row, complete to match left front, reversing shapings.

SLEEVES (both alike)
Cast on 34 (36: 38: 40: 42: 44) sts using 5mm (US 8) needles.
Beg with a K row, work in st st throughout as follows:
Work 12 rows, ending with a WS row.
Next row (RS): K3, M1, K to last 3 sts, M1, K3.
Working all increases as set by last row, inc 1 st at each end of 8th (8th: 8th: 10th: 8th: 8th) and every foll 8th (8th: 10th: 10th: 8th: 8th) row to 42 (42: 60: 62: 50: 50) sts, then on every foll 10th (10th: -: -: 10th: 10th) row until there are 56 (58: -: -: 66: 68) sts.

Cont straight until sleeve measures 49 (50: 51: 52: 53: 54) cm, ending with a WS row.
Shape top
Cast off 3 (3: 4: 4: 5: 5) sts at beg of next 2 rows. 50 (52: 52: 54: 56: 58) sts.
Dec 1 st at each end of next 3 rows, then on foll alt row, then on 2 foll 4th rows. 38 (40: 40: 42: 44: 46) sts.
Work 1 row.
Dec 1 st at each end of next and every foll alt row until 32 sts rem, then on foll 5 rows, ending with a WS row.
Cast off rem 22 sts.

MAKING UP
Press all pieces with a warm iron over a damp cloth.
Join both shoulder seams using back stitch or mattress stitch if preferred.
Left front tie
Cast on 12 sts using 5mm (US 8) needles.
Row 1 (RS): Knit.
Row 2: K2, P8, K2.
Rep last 2 rows until tie measures 89 (94: 99: 104: 109: 114) cm, ending with a WS row.
Cast off.
Right front tie
Work as given for left front tie but making this tie 105 (110: 115: 120: 125: 130) cm long. Attach end of ties to appropriate front opening edge, attaching top of tie level with start of front slope shaping. Join side seams, leaving side seams open below markers (for side seam openings) and leaving a small opening in right side seam level with tie (to thread left front tie through). Join sleeve seams. Insert sleeves into armholes.

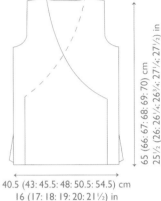

65 (66: 67: 68: 69: 70) cm
25½ (26: 26¼: 26¾: 27¼: 27½) in

40.5 (43: 45.5: 48: 50.5: 54.5) cm
16 (17: 18: 19: 20: 21½) in

49 (50: 51: 52: 53: 54) cm
19¼ (19¾: 20: 20½: 21: 21¼) in

INFORMATION

EXPERIENCE RATING

● for novice knitter
● ● for average knitter
● ● ● for experienced knitter

TENSION

Obtaining the correct tension is perhaps the single factor which can make the difference between a successful garment and a disastrous one. It controls both the shape and size of an article, so any variation, however slight, can distort the finished garment. We recommend that you knit a square in pattern and/or stocking stitch (depending on the pattern instructions) of perhaps 5 – 10 more stitches and 5 – 10 more rows than those given in the tension note. Mark out the central 10cm square with pins. If you have too many stitches to 10cm try again using thicker needles, if you have too few stitches to 10cm try again using finer needles. Once you have achieved the correct tension your garment will be knitted to the measurements indicated in the size diagram shown at the end of the pattern.

Please note, if you are unable to achieve the correct stitches and rows required, the stitches are more crucial as many patterns are knitted to length.

Keep an eye on your tension during knitting, especially if you're going back to work which has been put to one side for any length of time.

SIZING

The instructions are given for the smallest size. Where they vary, work the figures in brackets for the larger sizes. One set of figures refers to all sizes.

The size diagram with each pattern will help you decide which size to knit.

The measurements given on the size diagram are the actual size your garment should be when completed.

Measurements will vary from design to design because the necessary ease allowances have been made in each pattern to give your garment the correct fit, i.e. a loose-fitting garment will be several cm wider than a neat fitted one, a snug fitting garment may have no ease at all.

CHART NOTE

Some of our patterns include a chart. Each square on a chart represents a stitch and each line of squares a row of knitting. When working from a chart, unless otherwise stated, read odd rows (RS) from right to left and even rows (WS) from left to right. The key alongside each chart indicates how each stitch is worked.

FINISHING INSTRUCTIONS

It is the pressing and finishing which will transform your knitted pieces into a garment to be proud of.

PRESSING

Darn in ends neatly along the selvage edge. Follow closely any special instructions given on the pattern or ball band and always take great care not to over press your work.

Block out your knitting on a pressing ironing board, easing into shape and unless otherwise stated, press each piece using a warm iron over a damp cloth.

Tip: Attention should be given to ribs/edgings; if the garment is close fitting – steam the ribs gently so that the stitches fill out but stay elastic. Alternatively, if the garment is to hang straight then steam out to the correct shape.

Tip: Take special care to press the selvedge's as this will make sewing up both easier and neater.

Tip: If the ball band indicates that the fabric is not to be pressed, then cover the blocked-out fabric with a damp white cotton cloth and leaving it to stand will have the desired effect

CONSTRUCTION

Stitching Together

When stitching the pieces together, remember to match areas of texture very carefully where they meet. Use a seam stitch such as back stitch or mattress stitch for all main knitting seams and join all ribs and neckband with mattress stitch, unless otherwise stated.

Take extra care when stitching the edgings and collars around the back neck of a garment. They control the width of the back neck and if too wide the garment will be ill fitting and drop off the shoulders.

Knit back neck edgings only to the length stated in the pattern, even stretching it slightly if for example you are working in garter or horizontal rib stitch.

Stitch edgings/collars firmly into place using a back-stitch seam, easing-in the back neck to fit the collar/edging rather than stretching the collar/edging to fit the back neck.

CARE INSTRUCTIONS

Yarns

Follow the care instructions printed on each individual ball band. Where different yarns are used in the same garment, follow the care instructions for the more delicate one.

Buttons

We recommend that buttons are removed if your garment is to be machine washed.

INFORMATION

ABBREVIATIONS

K	knit
P	purl
K1b	knit 1 through back loop
st(s)	stitch(es)
inc	increas(e)(ing)
dec	decreas(e)(ing)
st st	stocking stitch (1 row K, 1 row P)
g st	garter stitch (K every row)
beg	begin(ning)
foll	following
rem	remain(ing)
rev st st	reverse stocking stitch (1 row P, 1 row K)
rep	repeat
alt	alternate
cont	continue
patt	pattern
tog	together
mm	millimetres
cm	centimetres
in(s)	inch(es)
RS	right side
WS	wrong side
sl 1	slip one stitch
psso	pass slipped stitch over
tbl	through back of loop
M1	make one stitch by picking up horizontal loop before next stitch and knitting into back of it
M1p	make one stitch by picking up horizontal loop before next stitch and purling into back of it
yfwd	yarn forward
yon	yarn over needle
yo	yarn over
yrn	yarn round needle
Cn	cable needle
-:	this dash indicates the particular instruction does not apply to your size

CROCHET

We are aware that crochet terminology varies from country to country. Please note we have used the English style in this publication.

CROCHET ABBREVIATIONS

ch chain
ss slip stitch
dc double crochet

Double crochet

01 Insert the hook into the work as indicated in the pattern, wrap the yarn over the hook and draw the yarn through the work only.

02 Wrap the yarn again and draw the yarn through both loops on the hook.

03 1 dc made.

BOBBLES

LALA & TIZZY
The bobble instructions in these two patterns create quite a large bobble, as seen on the photographed garment. If you prefer a smaller bobble, work as follows: (K1, P1, K1, P1) all into next st, turn, P4, turn, K4, turn, (P2tog) twice, turn, sl 1, K1, psso.
When working next row, knit into the back of the bobble st.
Please note that working the smaller bobbles may result in less yarn being used.

INDEX
the designs at a glance

NOVA
picture 27
pattern 57

ARIA
picture 29
pattern 60

AYA
picture 24
pattern 50

EILA
picture 31
pattern 58

FAIN		GLIDE		SWIRL	
picture	13 & 32	picture	16	picture	35 & 37
pattern	53	pattern	42	pattern	49

FLURRY		LALA		TIZZY	
picture	08	picture	19	picture	11
pattern	38	pattern	46	pattern	40

FLUTTER		QUIVER		WAVER	
picture	21	picture	22	picture	12 & 14
pattern	44	pattern	55	pattern	56